# CURRICULUM PLANNING WITH DESIGN LANGUAGE

*Curriculum Planning with Design Language* provides a streamlined, adaptable framework for using visual design terminology to conceptualize instructional design objectives, processes, and strategies. Drawing from instructional design theory, pattern language theory, and aesthetics, these ten course and unit design principles help educators break down and clarify their broader planning tasks and concerns. Written in clear, direct prose and rich with intuitive examples, this book showcases insights leading to effective curriculum design that will speak equally to pre-service and experienced educators.

**Ken Badley** teaches in the Department of Education at Mount Royal University, Canada, and serves as Professor of Education by Special Appointment at Tyndale University College, Canada. He recently completed nine years of service in the doctoral program in education at George Fox University, USA.

# CURRICULUM PLANNING WITH DESIGN LANGUAGE

## Building Elegant Courses and Units

*Ken Badley*

*Illustrations by Kristen Badley*

Routledge
Taylor & Francis Group

NEW YORK AND LONDON

First published 2019
by Routledge
711 Third Avenue, New York, NY 10017

and by Routledge
2 Park Square, Milton Park, Abingdon, Oxon, OX14 4RN

*Routledge is an imprint of the Taylor & Francis Group, an informa business*

*Library of Congress Cataloging-in-Publication Data*
Names: Badley, Kenneth Rea, 1951– author. | Badley, Kristen, illustrator.
Title: Curriculum planning with design language : building elegant courses and units / Ken Badley ; illustrations by Kristen Badley.
Description: New York : Routledge, 2019. | Includes bibliographical references and index.
Identifiers: LCCN 2018020445 (print) | LCCN 2018036369 (ebook) | ISBN 9781315146140 (eBook) | ISBN 9781138504714 (hbk) | ISBN 9781138504721 (pbk) | ISBN 9781315146140 (ebk)
Subjects: LCSH: Curriculum planning. | Instructional systems—Design.
Classification: LCC LB2806.15 (ebook) | LCC LB2806.15 .B34 2019 (print) | DDC 375/.001—dc23
LC record available at https://lccn.loc.gov/2018020445

ISBN: 978-1-138-50471-4 (hbk)
ISBN: 978-1-138-50472-1 (pbk)
ISBN: 978-1-315-14614-0 (ebk)

Typeset in Bembo and Stone Sans
by Florence Production Ltd, Stoodleigh, Devon, UK

To the generations of students who have taught me
what is written here

# CONTENTS

# PREFACE

Teaching is like working on five jigsaw puzzles simultaneously, with all the pieces in a single pile and no certainty that the photographs on the boxes accurately represent the pictures you are supposed to assemble. Teachers need to manage curriculum, instruction, and assessment while building a positive classroom climate and staying caught up with their administrative tasks. It would be simpler if teachers could work at these big five separately, and teacher-training programs do try to break them apart for the purposes of study, but real-world teaching requires that teachers go at all five at the same time. Somewhere in the middle of that pile of pieces are the needed components of good instruction. What works best with which students? What are the elements of a great class? What immutable laws, if there are any, govern how classes work and how students respond to instruction? Is direct instruction really as bad as its critics say? How does a teacher plan a unit?

For many teachers, that last question presents a sticky problem and is one of the reasons I wrote this book. Pre-service teachers I have worked with tell me that they know how to plan lessons but are not so sure about planning units. Some in-service teachers report that they just work through the textbook or they teach what they taught last year, rarely checking and possibly having forgotten the learning outcomes specified for the course or unit in question. In higher education, some simply show the PowerPoint slides provided to them by the textbook's publisher, pushing the *PgDn* key repeatedly until the semester ends. On the other hand, many teachers participate regularly, even weekly, in professional learning communities where they pool ideas and help each other plan instruction. Such is the range of approaches educators take to longer-range instructional planning. Various factors underwrite this range of practices and in this book I am more concerned to aid the teacher who wants to plan great units than to convert the person who should be replaced by a computer.

In *Awakening the Inner Eye*, Nel Noddings and Paul Shore call for educators to approach curriculum and instruction that starts with less defined objectives. They want educators to take intuition into account. I do not mention their work here because they suggest designing according to aesthetic principles (which they do not do) but because they ask educators to consider an approach other than what has become orthodoxy in our time. The approach I take here is not orthodox. Orthodoxy at this time implies starting with identifying the learning objectives, big questions, or big ideas, then deciding what kind of assessments would allow students to demonstrate that they have achieved the desired targets, then identifying what instruction would move students to those achievements. In this book, I say repeatedly that this approach makes complete sense, especially in comparison to simply pushing *PgDn* day after day so students can see PowerPoint slides provided by a textbook's publisher. But I also say that this approach does not go far enough. Like Noddings and Shore, I want us to rethink planning. Specifically, I believe we need to add a stage called design somewhere into the steps of what we now call *planning*.

This book has several roots. It grew initially out of the design philosophy of Christopher Alexander and then out of my reading of hundreds of other artists, designers, architects, and builders of bridges. It also started in a high-school social studies classroom where a student once blurted out that he had no idea how the unit we were studying fit into the course. I initially wondered what his problem was, and then realized it was my problem . . . for not making that connection clear. It also has roots in a third, deeply frustrating, place. At several points, my teaching responsibilities in education programs have included courses in program planning and instructional design for K–12 classrooms. Some of the textbooks available for these courses include complicated graphics about how planning works when the teacher has all the time in the world and all the students are in the top decile. In these books, my students and I saw flow charts with as many as 20 boxes, connected by arrows running in all directions. We saw so many acronyms that we wondered if we had accidentally begun reading a military manual. In short, to the extent I could understand these books, they presented a complicated and overly mechanistic view of planning that was, at the same time, very optimistic about educators' abilities to predict and control the outcomes of their work.

To the concerns I address in this book, those planning textbooks did not begin by having teachers pay attention to design. They began (appropriately) by having teachers identify the learning outcomes, then the assessments, then the instruction. However, many who recite that quick trio of steps as the key to good planning fail to explain how a teacher should decide what to do on the ninth day of the unit, which happens to be on the Thursday before a long weekend, or on the fifteenth day of the unit, a Wednesday in the middle of five straight weeks of instruction, each of which has five days in it. Classes on those two days may differ very markedly from each other. For one thing, student energy for learning will almost certainly be at a low ebb on the Thursday before a long weekend. And it could again be low on that mid-stretch Wednesday. Without questioning that teachers should take learning objectives into account (after all, that's why their jurisdictions pay them their salaries), my problem was and remains that planning models that start somewhere other than with design questions and do not take context into account will not lead to great units. Teachers are rushed and, to allude to John Holt's book title from long ago, they want to know what to do Monday. In-service teachers and my education students want a simplified planning model and process that works in their actual work weeks. It needs to be agile and it needs to work in the real classroom contexts within which students and teachers do their work.

Having complained about other books on planning, I now must register that this book is not intended as a how-to. In Chapters 3 to 12, I outline ten principles of good unit design and I note classroom applications for every one of those principles. I could argue (truthfully) that I have distilled these principles by observing great teachers over several decades. I also could argue (truthfully) that I have distilled these principles from careful study in design and architecture, noting again the significant influence of two books by Christopher Alexander, *A Pattern Language* and *The Timeless Way of Building*. For a book not intended as a how-to, I still provide one chapter that walks teachers step-by-step through the design of a unit plan. I have led a dozen workshops with in-service and pre-service teachers where individuals and teams as small as two and as large as eight have designed units in about two hours.

I wrote this book for teachers, whether in training or already in service. With that intended audience always in mind, I wrote in a warm tone, without a lot of reference apparatus. I use the pronouns "I" and "we" extensively because I believe that most educators (certainly the ones who will read this book) are, like me, trying to assemble these jigsaw puzzles. In this case, the educators looking in the jumble for the pieces on instruction are my special interest. In my view, we are in this together.

In recent decades, the assessment juggernaut has diminished teachers' sense of professional craft. Especially in K-12 education, teachers are told continually to focus on learning targets; classrooms have increasingly become places where only what can be counted counts. In this potentially toxic context, teachers need an antidote. With this book I want to inspire teachers to believe that in their educational work they can be professional designers, artists, and craftspeople who aim at something besides year-on-year growth targets. I want to help teachers aim at being great teachers who lead students into states of wonder about the amazing world in which they have found themselves. If I can simplify and bring more joy to educators' and students' work by helping teachers design rather than simply plan, and thereby make the structure of units more visible and their contents more powerful, I will be a happier man.

So, who is this book for? Obviously, teachers in training. But in a Kentopian fantasy, I hope that it serves as interesting reading for anyone concerned about education and how we might recover a sense of craft in a time when the values of mass production have again begun to invade schools. I wrote this for the pre-service teacher trying to understand the planning process and for veteran teachers who need to rejuvenate their program. I think about colleagues of mine who have taught for two or three decades and I hope they could pick this book up and say, "He has given me new ideas. He has made me think in a new way about curriculum." Other veteran teachers may simply find that I describe what they have been doing all along. If the principles I describe here are indeed distilled from observing great classroom practice, then that may well happen. I hope that someone still completing their undergraduate degree in education or a teacher in her first or second year of teaching could pick this book up and at the end of it say, "this helped me see curriculum in a way that I don't think I could have done otherwise."

The argument I make in what follows will feel initially as if I have set out to destabilize the planning process. At the time of writing, most in the educational community—whether educators themselves or professors in places where teachers are taught—have largely agreed that planning should start with the learning outcomes and work backwards from there. In fact, that is precisely how I plan my teaching. But approaching this planning task first as a design task, or preceding the planning with designing, implies that I frame my planning differently from how I would if I were thinking of planning only with reference to what my students know and what I would like them to know later.

Since at least Dewey's time, educators have asked whether instruction should be shaped more by psychological questions such as "Who are the learners?" and "How do they learn?" or by epistemological questions such as "What are the contents?" and "What are the structures of the disciplines?" Some refer to this debate as the "I teach students" vs. "I teach subjects" debate. I will come back to this debate in the book but for now want to suggest that it misfigures things, in at least two ways. First, why does it have to be either this or that, when, in fact, we need to take both psychological and epistemological factors into account; we teach both students and subjects. Second, and to my concern about design, the debate ignores the character—or the shape, if you like—of the learning contents themselves. Unless we attend to the design of instruction, the subjects-students debate will miss the point. We need to start with design.

*Ken Badley*
*Calgary, April 2018*

# ACKNOWLEDGMENTS

Many people contributed to my thinking and helped me in the production of this book. My Calgary editor, Hannah Ayer, turned lead into gold at several points in the writing process. My daughter, Kristen Badley, from Edmonton, produced all the graphics, managed the photographs and permissions, fed me ideas, and, as far as I know, worked patiently with me throughout the process. Both Hannah and Kristen did much more than they should ever have had to do. I wish to acknowledge the support of members of Team Ken who organized research, read the proposal or chapters, copy-edited, or simply told me to keep at it. Team Ken includes B. Ali, B. Ashlin-Mayo, J. R. Badley, K. J. Badley, G. Loewen-Thomas, K. McGougan, and G. Sehorn, S. Steeg-Thornhill, and T. Tucker. Although her name also appears as a member of Team Ken, I wish to acknowledge especially the support and patience of my wife, K. Jo-Ann Badley, who supported me throughout the years it took to bring this project to life. Thanks to several organizations and corporations who permitted the use of their images, as well as the many friends who offered or contributed photographs, including W. Coleman, A. Demaurex, J. Kopfová, P. Marriott, C. Nelson, J.-F. Noble, J. Smith, B. Zutter, and especially Joe Reimer (joereimer.com). I thank the roughly 100 teachers and students who attended my workshops to help me refine the concepts, especially D. Cloutier and K. MacIsaac, both of whom simply kept coming back. Daniel Schwartz, my editor at Routledge, guided me patiently through the process of writing the manuscript and moving it through the production stages. I thank the three anonymous reviewers who read the proposal in late in 2016 and early 2017. I thank Tamsyn Hopkins and her team at Florence Production in Devon, who worked patiently on the book's production and Sarah Adams, Production Editor at Routledge. Finally, I wish to acknowledge the influence of architect, Christopher Alexander. I first learned of his work in a *Wired Magazine* article in March 2004 and knew instantly that the principles he worked on throughout his career applied to curriculum and instruction. In the years since that *Wired* article, I have read his entire corpus. He has inspired me and shaped my thinking profoundly. This book would literally not have come into being without him.

**FIGURE 1.1** A Roman aqueduct depends on design elements

# 1

# DESIGNING INSTRUCTION

Teachers who give some time to design units before they start to plan instruction can simplify and streamline the planning process and increase their students' self-efficacy. In this book, I offer ten design principles which, taken together, form a kind of language for unit design. Implementing any of these principles alone would help produce more elegant units and lead to improvements in student learning. Taken and used together, these principles form a powerful framework for unit design.

This chapter begins with a brief review of teachers' typical approaches to planning instruction. I follow that by making a distinction between two important concepts, design and planning. While these two concepts are obviously connected, they need to be distinguished very carefully for my purposes here. In the third major section, I trace the immigration of design thinking into education, a process that divides roughly into four periods.

## How Teachers Plan Instruction

Teachers take a host of factors into account when they plan instruction. First and obviously, they need to help their students learn what, for lack of a better term, I will call the *curriculum*. This learning ranges from "make sense of problems and persevere in solving them" (grades 3–5 mathematics in Massachusetts) to understanding "What makes a community?" and "How do I fit in?" (grade 1 social studies in Alberta). Planning must take into account the published curriculum standards but, in a sense, these standards are just the beginning. Teachers need to help students learn 21st-century skills, although the jury has not yet agreed on precisely what those are. From one source or another—perhaps these mandates are simply in the air that teachers breathe—they hear that they must also be front-line responders to society's need for students to be technologically proficient, or familiar with anti-bullying strategies. Schools shoulder some of the burden for sex education and for raising environmental awareness. Presumably, teachers are to incorporate all this teaching and learning into the courses and units already on the books, courses such as social studies and mathematics.

Teachers also plan instruction in light of several realities related to the calendar. They work within the constraints of an annual calendar and several national holidays. School jurisdictions and individual schools set holiday breaks, as well as dates for teacher professional development, teacher conventions, parent conferences, staff meetings, assemblies, sports days, and even school concerts and plays.

In addition to accommodating all these practical and logistical concerns, teachers must take learning theory into account in their planning; they must consider what students already know and scaffold new learning onto old knowledge. By the day they graduate from their teaching program, new teachers will have heard repeatedly about learning styles and multiple intelligences. During their various in-school placements, they will likely already have met students who have their own Individual Learning Plan or Individual Education Plan because of a learning disability or behavioural tendency. They may also have worked with talented and gifted (TAG) students, some of whom are mainstreamed and others of whom are pulled out of class for daily or weekly special programming. To my point, when they plan instruction, teachers need to take a range of idiomatic concerns into consideration.

In the upper grades and in higher education, educators must consider the conceptual structures within a field of study. Academic disciplines comprise networks and hierarchies of concepts that stand in various kinds of relationships to each other. Students must understand some concepts before they can learn others. In chemistry, *valence* precedes *compound*. In mathematics, *integer* precedes *fraction*. In social studies, *government* precedes *parliamentary democracy*. In the academic disciplines, the networks and hierarchies of concepts, the accepted tests for evidence, and the canons and landmarks—taken together—comprise a disciplined way of viewing an aspect of the world. Teachers in secondary and higher education induct their students into the disciplines and into those disciplined ways of examining the world (Hirst & Peters, 1970). By necessity, educators at these levels must consider the respective disciplinary structures when they plan their instruction.

Finally, legislative factors impinge on teachers' planning. Teachers do their work in light of a *Schools Act* or *Education Act* passed by their respective nation (if there is a national education system) or by their state, canton, or province (if the nation's constitution passes the responsibility for education down). Those respective Acts shape most aspects of the operation of schools and of teachers' professional work. Teachers need to take very serious account of this legislation because it literally governs their work. In addition to that overarching legal framework, school districts add their own policies, determine new mandates for their schools, and declare local initiatives. Finally, individual schools add to the mix.

In summary, when planning instruction, teachers take a host of factors into account. Both pre-service teachers and in-service teachers know about these many necessary considerations. This is a theme that runs through the research on how teachers plan (Martin, 1990; Masterman, 2009) and it partly explains why teachers tend to concern themselves more with the immediate questions of pedagogical content and resource materials than with design principles. Given the range of factors teachers must consider when planning and the number of classes per day that they must plan for, no one should be surprised that in planning instruction some teachers look mainly to the textbook and to teaching materials they have available from previous years. John Holt's book *What Do I Do Monday?* (1995) has resonated with teachers over several decades not just because it is packed with teaching ideas but because its title catches what, for so many teachers, is the most pressing question. No one should be surprised about the growth in popularity of the work of Jay McTighe and Grant Wiggins and their idea of planning *backwards by design* (1999, 2005, 2013). In the rush to get ready for each day, one can easily focus more on what one's students will study— on what the class will "do"—and forget to ask about the learning outcomes one is aiming at. In fact, at its worst, this focus on what one will do on a given day can be reduced to "What pages of my binder will the class copy down today?" or even "Which PowerPoint deck from the textbook publisher will I click through today?"

McTighe and Wiggins have reminded generations of teachers to identify the desired learning outcomes first, then to ask what assessments would indicate that students have met those outcomes, and then to ask what instruction and activities would enable students to succeed on those assessments. The backwards-by-design planning model makes complete sense. One almost wishes McTighe and Wiggins had never had to point it out.

In light of the planning and instructional pressures on teachers (which I treat again in Chapter 12), no one should be surprised that most teachers give little thought to design, and that they go straight to planning (Kerr, 1983; Koh & Chai, 2016; Koh, Chai, Wong, & Hong, 2016). Planning is obviously necessary. In planning, the teacher makes decisions about what to teach. But planning, by itself, offers no principles about fitting instructional plans into the rhythms of the teacher's own life, about the energy teachers and students have for learning on any given day, about the effects of repetition and variety, or about the need to breathe somewhere in the middle of a six-week stretch of classes with no long weekends. Even those who adhere most closely to *backwards by design* or *universal design for learning* still need to project how things will flow from day to day and week to week. What I call planning does not offer much to the teacher needing to make those bigger projections. What I call design addresses that need directly. Because these terms both figure centrally in discussion of teachers' work, and because many people treat them as synonyms, I will now distinguish the two at some length.

## Two Concepts: Design and Planning

The previous section included a possibly intimidating catalogue of factors and forces that teachers must take into account when they plan instruction. As I noted previously, I believe that teachers who engage in design before they start to plan not only simplify and streamline their planning process but also increase their students' self-efficacy. Before we dive too deeply into a discussion of this approach, I must distinguish what I mean by *design* from what I mean by *planning*. A majority of participants in the planning conversation employ these two terms interchangeably, their usage represented by the Venn diagram on the left side of Figure 1.2. Reading a few pages in most books whose titles include phrases such as *unit design*, *curriculum design*, *instructional design*, and *course design* will reveal that the authors of those books are writing about planning, whether it is from day to day, week to week, or semester to semester. In essence, those who speak of design this way are asking these questions: "Given that students need to learn these things, what should they study first, second, and third? What must be included and what may be omitted?"

Using the word *design* to designate planning—what I call undifferentiated usage—is neither right nor wrong and I cannot legislate other people's linguistic preferences. My purpose in this section is only to note common usage and not to criticize those who speak of design in an undifferentiated way. That said, I am among the minority of users who would prefer the Venn diagram on the right side of Figure 1.2, that is, who do not equate the two but who instead want to restrict the word *design* to its artistic, aesthetic sense. For my purposes here, I will stipulate definitions of both terms and use them throughout

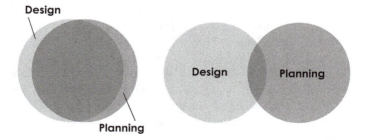

**FIGURE 1.2** Venn diagrams showing varying degrees of semantic conflation between the concepts of design and planning

the book, taking care to speak of design only in a differentiated way, that is, as distinct from planning.

Let me offer the two stipulated definitions. By *planning*, I mean the process of deciding what the students and their teacher will do in a given day, week, month, or term. For example, a university instructor might plan to work through the syllabus and lead a tour of the course wiki on the first day of the semester, and plan on the second day to give the first of three lectures on the major upheavals that ended the Medieval Period. In an elementary classroom, a teacher might plan to have the students fill out the first two columns of a three-column KWL sheet (what I **K**now, what I **W**ould like to learn, what I **L**earned) as her introduction to a new unit on electricity and magnetism. If she were familiar with *Visible Learning* and Harvard's Project Zero (2013), she might favor an adaptation of the KWL sheet and plan to ask her students to fill in the first column with what they **T**hink they know. In these examples, teachers are planning what they and their students will do in class, in this case, on the first day of a new unit. I will use the word *planning* throughout the book to designate this kind of activity.

Of the two terms, *design* presents us with more problems, the first of which may be that the design field itself has struggled to define this key term (Barab & Squire, 2004; Cross, 1999; O'Donnell, 2004; Pirolli, 1991; Reigeluth, 1999; Reigeluth, Beatty, & Myers, 2016; Schatz, 2003). As an educator, not a professional designer, I will not try to solve here what the design community has failed to solve. However, the concept needs clarification for there to be productive conversation about the design thinking that I believe needs to precede planning. With the word *design* I refer to questions of form and shape, symmetry, beauty, line, coherence, elegance, and even accessibility by students. In the chapters that follow, I restrict *design* to the process of framing unit and course planning aesthetically. Framed aesthetically, planning is preceded by questions such as these: What simple, elegant structure underlies this unit (Chapter 12)? How can

**FIGURE 1.3** Distinguishing the three concepts of design, planning, and preparation and illustrating how each layer rests on those below

I reveal that structure to students so they can see that all the parts of the unit cohere (Chapter 6)? How do I introduce the most difficult concepts in ways that don't intimidate my students (Chapter 10)? How do I combine repetition, variety, and contrast in ways that engage students (Chapter 9)? These are design questions, and after I introduce the ten design principles in Chapter 2, I explore each one in detail in Chapters 3 through 12. Throughout those chapters, I restrict the word *design* to its differentiated sense, the sense tied to the fields of art, architecture, aesthetics, and design.

Within the concept of *planning*, it is also necessary to distinguish between unit planning and day-to-day preparation. Many educators use these two words interchangeably, but at points in this discussion I will need to distinguish between them. When teachers prepare to inaugurate a new lesson or unit, they plan, prepare materials, estimate times needed to complete tasks, and so on. To use a construction metaphor, this stage is more like the building phase in construction. An architect has already designed the structure. The contractor has already worked with the owner to negotiate the costs and construction schedule (the metaphorical equivalent of unit planning). After all this work, the contractor, crew, and sub-trades build the building. The myriad details involved in the building stage parallel the details involved in day-to-day instructional planning. In the same way that many educators conflate the concepts of design and planning, they also use *planning* and *day-to-day preparation* interchangeably. Distinguishing these two stages or concepts is not essential to the argument I make in this book, but the distinction is helpful, and I will use both concepts carefully.

In the next section of this chapter and in Chapter 2, I introduce two more important terms, *principles* and *patterns*. These words both figure importantly in the design conversation and we need clarity about their respective meanings from the outset.

## Pattern Languages and Instructional Design

The design framework I propose in this book has a brief but interesting history, which I will review here in four stages. The first stage involves the architectural work of Christopher Alexander, who taught for many years at the University of California at Berkeley. Specifically, I note his concept of a *pattern language*. In the second stage, software developers in the late 1980s and especially in the 1990s began to appropriate Alexander's pattern language idea, believing that writing code could be simplified if knowledge could be encapsulated in design patterns. The next step involved instructors in computer science, who, aware of how software developers had adopted Alexander's concept of patterns, proposed patterns for course websites and then computer science instruction more generally. Finally, the idea of patterns and pattern languages began to migrate over to instruction in general, a migration still in process and still somewhat tentative.

Many others have traced this history, some at book length, and I will not go into detail here on matters dealt with in depth elsewhere.

Christopher Alexander was born in Vienna in 1936 but raised in England. He took his first degree at Trinity College, Cambridge University, graduating in 1958. After completing his doctorate at Harvard, he published his dissertation as *Notes on the Synthesis of Form* (1964). In 1972, the American Institute of Architects awarded him a gold medal for this research, but he later distanced himself from this work, concluding that he had reduced architectural decisions about design and beauty to unnatural, complicated mathematical algorithms. During his decades of teaching at Berkeley, he adopted the view that what he called *design patterns* were theoretical descriptions of the relationships between the elements of places that people everywhere love or find beautiful. For example, almost anyone drinking coffee in the square of a centuries-old village or town in France will have immediate affection for that square. Alexander's approach was to ask about the features of that square that make its occupants feel that affection.

Alexander's best-known works were *A Pattern Language*, which he wrote with several doctoral students (1977), and *The Timeless Way of Building* (Alexander, 1979). By the phrase *pattern language*, Alexander refers to the way that a number of patterns work together, like the way the parts of spoken language work together by following the rules of grammar and syntax. The most thorough statement of his evolving philosophy appeared in our own century in the four volumes of *The Nature of Order* (2002a, 2002b, 2004, 2005). In *A Pattern Language*, Alexander presented 253 principles or patterns. In the volumes that comprise *The Nature of Order*, he reduces his approach to just fifteen patterns. At the time of this writing, Alexander's latest work (with two others) appeared as *The Battle for the Life and Beauty of the Earth: A Struggle Between Two World-Systems* (Alexander, Neis, & Alexander, 2012). The title makes clear that, in his ninth decade, Alexander still has fire in his bones.

Based largely on what Alexander offered in the 1970s in *A Pattern Language and The Timeless Way of Building*, software developers became interested in the idea of patterns and pattern languages. Developers made some efforts in the late 1980s to develop a pattern language for writing software, but these efforts garnered little attention at the time. Momentum increased in the early 1990s. In an initiative led by Coad, North and Mayfield (1995) and Gamma, Helm, Johnson and Vlissides (1995), a number of software developers began to use Alexander's principles to provide a framework for writing computer code. These two pioneering teams later formed a coalition, Pattern Languages of Program Design (PLOP, www.hillside.net/past-plop-conferences). The PLOP coalition, part of the Hillside Group, meets annually, has invited Alexander to speak in person, and uses his concept of a pattern language to simplify and add elegance to the writing of code. Many have explored at greater length the story of how the software industry adopted Alexander's idea of patterns (Appleton, 2000; Coplien, 1996, 2001; Fowler, 1997; Rising, 1999, 2007, 1998).

From software, patterns took a short jump to computer science instruction, another story others have told in detail (Goodyear et al., 2004; Kohls, 2011, 2013; Retalis, Georgiakakis, & Dimitriadis, 2006; Warburton & Mor, 2015; Warburton, Mor, & Koskinen, 2015). Intuitively, it makes sense that computer science educators might hear first what the software community had discovered to be so useful. But the next step—the uptake of patterns into the non-online educational community—was not so quick. Numerous writers have noted the resistance to or slow uptake of pattern approaches to instruction. One suggestion is that some online educators focused too much on the technical side and not enough on the pedagogical side. As is often the case, the technology available determines the shape that instruction finally takes, and ultimately may even undermine the instruction (Mouasher & Lodge, 2016).

Another group, known as the *pedagogical patterns project*, grew out of Alexander's work (Magnusson, 2006; Sharp, Manns, & Eckstein, 2003). People pushing for patterns originally hoped to be able to share instructional design knowledge with a standard set of protocols or formats that would simplify dissemination and increase understanding (McAndrew, Goodyear, & Dalziel, 2006; Mor, 2011; Mor, Mellar, Warburton, & Winters, 2014; Mor & Warburton, 2015; Mor & Winters, 2008). This wish paralleled the original movement in software, in which developers viewed patterns as a compact and efficient means of sharing good practice. Some followers of Alexander prefer to speak of *design languages*, as frameworks broader than pedagogical patterns (Seo & Gibbons, 2003). As I have done several times already in this chapter, I will decline to repeat work that others have offered elsewhere.

Separate from those who followed Alexander and wanted to develop patterns, a movement known as Instructional Design (with intentional upper-case letters) grew in the 1980s and 1990s. It attracted some adherents in online education but ultimately failed to influence many face-to-face educators. Some researchers have speculated that ID failed to catch on because its proponents did not focus enough on the practical issues of course design faced by ordinary teachers (Moallem, 1998; Streibel, 1991). This accords with my own reading experience in ID; with reference to one book about ID, I noted that I felt like I was being asked to get a PhD in physics when all I wanted to do was add an outlet in my garage. Others have conjectured that emphasis on written material combined with a shortage of visual material rendered ID less accessible to general audiences (Stubbs, 2006; Stubbs & Gibbons, 2008). Still others have suggested that a kind of technical rationality took over ID, ignoring the creative, divergent, and intuitive processes that are involved when living beings interact (Rowland, 1993, 2004; Wittmann, 1995) and attempting to reduce instruction to a set of routines that computers could manage (Parker, 2000; Parrish, 2005, 2009).

Another movement known as instructional design (this one with intentional lower-case letters) evolved in the 1980s and 1990s, separate from both the patterns movement and from ID. One useful history of instructional design is that by Koh, Chai, Wong, and Hong (2016), although they tend to use the word *design* in its undifferentiated sense. Finally, from the late 1990s on, design studies became another area of research in education, although like the field of design itself it has struggled to identify its focus, among other issues (O'Donnell, 2004; Shavelson, Phillips, Towne, & Feuer, 2003). In short, interest has grown in designing—not simply planning—instruction, but that growth has been bumpy and characterized by a dearth of communication or agreement on what approaches might work best.

An interesting story of one university's exploration of pattern languages bears telling here. In the late 1980s, with encouragement from one professor, the University of Cincinnati School of Education investigated the possibility of using *A Pattern Language* to redesign its teacher education program (Yinger, 1989; Yinger & Hendricks-Lee, 1992). The idea never came to fruition. When I queried Yinger, the idea's sponsor, regarding the reasons for non-adoption, he answered that the faculty recognized that pattern language offered an elegant way to conceptualize the School of Education's curriculum and program, but faculty were more comfortable with older and more familiar frameworks (Yinger, 2008). The experience of the University of Cincinnati is as much a metaphor as an isolated story. For most people, pattern languages and the idea of a pattern language remain unfamiliar territory.

## Design and Instructional Design

Several titles have appeared recently that indicate that change may be in the wind. Some of these accord quite closely with my own stipulated definition of instructional design, others differ.

Diana Laurillard titled her book *Teaching as a Design Science: Building Pedagogical Patterns for Learning and Technology* (2012). Despite its title, *Teaching as a Design Science* does not deal directly with the design principles that drive design and architecture. She makes reference to some of the software writers who found Christopher Alexander's ideas helpful and, to her credit, she addresses the questions of what learners bring to the classroom and of how they experience curriculum and instruction. The book's focus is on how teachers can use technology to enhance student learning and, despite her choice of title, Laurillard seems to miss the foundations of design, settling instead for familiar principles of course and curriculum planning.

The second book, *Pedagogical Patterns: Advice for Educators*, was self-published on Amazon by the Pedagogical Patterns Editorial Board (Bergin et al., 2012). These educators have explicitly recognized their debt to Christopher Alexander, mentioning him often and formatting their book similarly to his *A Pattern Language*, but the patterns they offer are simply the same principles of sound instruction that every teacher training program offers its pre-service teachers, principles such as encourage teamwork and build on past experience. This group

**FIGURE 1.4** Some of the many titles relate to instructional design

uses the word *patterns* in somewhat the same way that the software writers I already mentioned use it: repeated practices that give structure to classrooms and teaching. However, despite using Alexander's work after a fashion, they do not address the foundational questions of course design as design; nor do they explain or illustrate the patterns Alexander himself identified.

Two more recent titles warrant mention here. In *An Architectural Approach to Instructional Design*, Andrew S. Gibbons (2014) gives a couple pages to the work of Christopher Alexander but develops his model of course design largely on the foundation of Stewart Brand's concept of layers from *How Buildings Learn* (1994). Although I do not use his framework here, Brand's idea of six "S" words, or layers (site, structure, skin, services, space plan, stuff), contains insight for curriculum and instructional designers (Figure 1.5). I have watched students in several classes struggle to agree about what parts of the school system match each level in Brand's assessment of how buildings work. I have yet to see a group of educators agree regarding which layers of Brand's framework match which aspects of education, but we always enjoy rich conversation as we try to persuade each other of our respective views. His use of Brand aside, Gibbons builds his model for curriculum and instruction as a whole largely from his experience in teaching online courses in software development. By using Brand's concept of layers, he succeeds in shining fresh light on one dimension of curriculum but more light is needed. On reading this new title by Gibbons, I became more convinced that we need design approaches to curriculum and instructional design. Also, Gibbons further persuaded me (and he persuaded Routledge) that educators are ready to begin thinking about course design as design. Until Gibbons, no one had offered educators an aesthetic approach to curriculum and course design and I recommend his work to anyone wanting to engage further in the instructional design conversation.

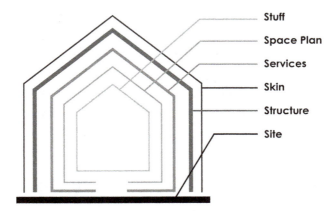

**FIGURE 1.5** Stewart Brand's understanding of the six layers in a building

## Why Write this Book?

My pre-service teachers remind me regularly that they find planning a lesson to be a daunting task. They also tell me that course and unit planning present their own challenges. I tell them that they will get better at it, that it becomes easier with time, and that it also becomes easier if they design first. In-service teachers remind me that planning and executing their classroom program month-to-month and year-to-year are tiring work. I cannot tell them that they will get better at it or that it will become easier with time. Even the veterans with the natural gifts of teaching that van Manen called *tact* struggle with weariness (1991). It is for teachers, whether already in service or in preparation, that I have written this book. In the Foreword, I noted that I first came across the work of Christopher Alexander and the idea of a pattern language in 2004. In the years since then, I have implemented the ideas I present here in my own secondary, undergraduate, graduate and doctoral courses. As I have offered these principles to both pre-service teachers and in-service teachers in workshops, I have heard many say that approaching planning by designing first actually simplifies the planning process.

Simplifying planning by starting with design is not the only reason to approach instructional planning with a pattern language. The second reason is likely more important: students feel more in control of their learning when their teachers and professors show them the big picture, especially if that big picture is simple and elegant. Jesse Schell, a game designer, claims that designers should look at game design through various lenses, ranging from psychology to mathematics, to puzzle design, and even to theme park design (2008). The same could be said of course and unit design. We have focused appropriately on learning theory, the structure of disciplines, learning outcomes, assessment, and a host of other factors. But perhaps we have not focused enough on how students experience instruction and how their self-efficacy fluctuates in relation to their own degree of understanding of the metaphorical—curricular and instructional—places they occupy at any point in our classes. We can address their need, in part at least, by attending to design itself. It is time we did so.

## References

Alexander, C. (1964). *Notes on the synthesis of form.* Cambridge, MA: Harvard University Press.

Alexander, C. (1979). *The timeless way of building.* New York: Oxford University Press.

Alexander, C. (2002a). *The phenomenon of life: The nature of order (volume 1).* Berkeley, CA: The Center for Environmental Structure.

Alexander, C. (2002b). *The process of creating life: The nature of order (volume 2).* Berkeley, CA: The Center for Environmental Structure.

Alexander, C. (2004). *The luminous ground: The nature of order (volume 4).* Berkeley, CA: The Center for Environmental Structure.

Alexander, C. (2005). *A vision of the living world: The nature of order (volume 3).* Berkeley, CA: The Center for Environmental Structure.

Alexander, C., Ishikawa, S., Silverstein, M., Jacobson, M., Fiksdahl-King, I., & Angel, S. (1977). *A pattern language: Towns, buildings, construction.* New York: Oxford University Press.

Alexander, C., Neis, H., & Alexander, M. M. (2012). *The battle for the life and beauty of the earth: A struggle between two world-systems.* New York: Oxford University Press.

Appleton, B. (2000). Patterns and software: Essential concepts and terminology. Retrieved from http://csis.pace.edu/~grossman/dcs/Patterns%20and%20Software-%20Essential%20Concepts%20and%20Terminology.pdf.

Barab, S., & Squire, K. (2004). Design-based research: Putting a stake in the ground. *Journal of the Learning Sciences,* 13(1), 1–14.

Bergin, J., Eckstein, J., Manns, M. L., Sharp, H., Marquardt, K., Chandler, J., . . . Wallingford, E. (Eds.). (2012). *Pedagogical patterns: Advice for educators.* Amazon CreateSpace.

Brand, S. (1994). *How buildings learn: What happens after they're built.* New York: Viking.

Coad, P., North, D., & Mayfield, M. (1995). *Object models: Strategies, patterns and applications.* Englewood Cliffs, NJ: Yourdon Press (Prentice-Hall).

Coplien, J. O. (1996). *Software patterns.* London: SIGS.

Coplien, J. O. (2001). A pattern definition: Software patterns. Retrieved from http://hillside.net/patterns/definition.html.

Cross, N. (1999). Design research: A disciplined conversation. *Design Issues,* 15(2), 5–10.

Fowler, M. (1997). *Analysis patterns: Reusable object models.* Reading, MA: Addison-Wesley.

Gamma, E., Helm, R., Johnson, R., & Vlissides, J. (1995). *Design patterns.* Lebanon, IN: Addison-Wesley.

Gibbons, A. S. (2014). *An architectural approach to instructional design.* New York: Routledge.

Goodyear, P., Avgeriou, P., Baggetun, R., Bartoluzzi, S., Regalis, S., Ronteltap, F., & Rusman, E. (2004). *Towards a pattern language for networked learning.* Paper presented at the Conference for Networked Learning, Lancaster, England. www.rug.nl/research/portal/en/publications/towards-a-pattern-language-for-networked-learning(138e7703-7a90-4dc7-bf9f-432e4fb9e7b1).html!null.

Harvard University. (2013). *Making learning visible*. Retrieved from www.pz.harvard.edu/projects/making-learning-visible.

Hirst, P., & Peters, R. S. (1970). *The logic of education*. London: Routledge.

Holt, J. (1995). *Why do I do Monday?* Portsmouth, NH: Boynton/Cook.

Kerr, S. T. (1983). *Inside the black box: Making design decisions for instruction*. Paper presented at the Association for Educational Communications and Technology, Dallas, TX.

Koh, J., & Chai, C. S. (2016). Seven design frames that teachers use when considering technological pedagocial content knowledge. *Computers and Education*, 102, 244–257.

Koh, J., Chai, C. S., Wong, B., & Hong, H.-Y. (2016). *Design thinking for education: Conceptions and applications in teaching and learning*. New York: Springer.

Kohls, C. (2011). Patterns as an analysis framework to document and foster excellent e-learning designs. In C. Kohls & J. Wedekind (Eds.), *Investigations of e-learning patterns: Context factors, problems, and solutions* (pp. 19–40). Hershey, NY: ICI Global.

Kohls, C. (2013). *The theories of design patterns and their practical implications exemplified for e-learning patterns*. (Doctoral dissertation), Catholic University of Eichstatt-Ingolstadt, Eichstatt, Germany. Retrieved from https://opus4.kobv.de/opus4-ku-eichstaett/frontdoor/index/index/docId/158.

Laurillard, D. (2012). *Teaching as a design science: Building pedagogical patterns for learning and technology*. New York: Routledge.

Magnusson, E. (2006). *Pegagogical patterns: A method to capture best practices in teaching and learning*. Paper presented at the LTHs pedagogiska inspirationskonferens (The Pedagogical Inspiration Conference at the Faculty of Engineering, Lund University), Lund, Sweden.

Martin, B. L. (1990). Teachers' planning processes: Does ISD make a difference. *Performance Improvement Quarterly*, 3(4), 53–73.

Masterman, E. (2009). Capturing teachers' experience of learning design through case studies. *Distance Education*, 30(2), 223–238.

McAndrew, P., Goodyear, P., & Dalziel, J. (2006). Patterns, designs and activities: Unifying descriptions of learning structures. *International Journal of Learning Technology*, 2(2–3), 216–242.

McTighe, J., & Wiggins, G. (1999). *Understanding by design handbook*. Alexandria, VA: Association for Supervision and Curriculum Development.

McTighe, J., & Wiggins, G. (2005). *Understanding by design (2nd ed.)*. Alexandria, VA: Association for Supervision and Curriculum Development.

McTighe, J., & Wiggins, G. (2013). *Essential questions: Opening doors to student understanding*. Alexandria, VA: ACSD.

Moallem, M. (1998). An expert teacher's thinking and teaching and instructional design models and principles: An ethnographic study. *ETR&D*, 46(2), 37–64.

Mor, Y. (2011). *Design narratives: An intuitive scientific form for capturing design knowledge*. Paper presented at the the 6th Chais conference on Instructional Technologies Research, Ra'anana, Israel.

Mor, Y., Mellar, H., Warburton, S., & Winters, N. (Eds.). (2014). *Practical design patterns for teaching and learning with technology*. Boston, MA: Sense.

Mor, Y., & Warburton, S. (2015). Practical patterns for active and collaborative MOOCs: Checkpoints, fish bowl, and see-do-share. *eLearning Papers*, 42, 48–56.

Mor, Y., & Winters, N. (2008). Participatory design in open education: A workshop model for developing a pattern language. *Journal of Interactive Media in Education*, 2008(1), Art. 12.

Mouasher, A., & Lodge, J. M. (2016). The search for pedagogical dynamism: Design patterns and the unselfconscious process. *Educational Technology and Society*, 19(2), 274–285.

O'Donnell, A. M. (2004). A commentary on design research. *Educational Psychologist*, 39(4), 255–260.

Parker, K. (2000). *Art, science and the importance of aesthetics in instructional design*. Doctoral course paper. University of San Francisco, School of Education. San Francisco, CA.

Parrish, P. E. (2005). Embracing the aesthetics of instructional design. Educational Technology, 45(2), 16–25.

Parrish, P. E. (2009). Aesthetic principles for instructional design. *Educational Technology Research and Development*, 57(4), 511–528.

Pirolli, P. (1991). Computer-aided instructional design systems. In H. Burns, J. Parlett, & C. Redfield (Eds.), *Intelligent tutoring systems: Evolution in design* (pp. 105–125). Hillsdale, NJ: Lawrence Erlbaum Associates.

Reigeluth, C. M. (1999). What is instructional design theory and how is it changing? In C. M. Reigeluth (Ed.), *Instructional design theories and models: A new paradigm of instructional theory* (Vol. 2, pp. 5–29). Mahwah, NJ: Lawrence Erlbaum Associates.

Reigeluth, C. M., Beatty, B. J., & Myers, R. D. (2016). *Instructional-design theories and models, Volume IV: The learner-centred paradigm of education*. New York: Routledge.

Retalis, S., Georgiakakis, P., & Dimitriadis, Y. (2006). Eliciting design patterns for e-learning systems. *Computer Science Education*, 16(2), 105–118.

Rising, L. (1999). Patterns: A way to reuse expertise. *IEEE Communications Magazine*, 37(4), 34–36.

Rising, L. (2007). Understanding the power of abstraction in patterns. *IEEE Software*, 24(4), 46–51.

Rising, L. (Ed.) (1998). *The patterns handbook: Technique, strategies, and applications*. Cambridge: Cambridge University Press.

Rowland, G. (1993). Design and instructional design. *Educational Technology Research and Development*, 41(1), 79–91.

Rowland, G. (2004). Shall we dance? A design epistemology for organizational learning performance. *Educational Technology Research and Development*, 52(1), 33–48.

Schatz, S. (2003). A matter of design: A proposal to encourage the evolution of design in instructional design. *Performance Improvement Quarterly*, 16(4), 59–73.

Schell, J. (2008). *The art of game design: A book of lenses*. Boston, MA: Elsevier/Morgan Kaufmann.

Seo, K. K., & Gibbons, A. S. (2003). Design languages: A powerful medium for communicating designs. *Educational Technology*, 43(6), 43–46.

Sharp, H., Manns, M. L., & Eckstein, J. (2003). Evolving pedagogical patterns: The work of the pedagogical patterns project. *Computer Science Education*, 13(4), 315–330.

Shavelson, R. J., Phillips, D. C., Towne, L., & Feuer, M. J. (2003). On the science of education design studies, 32, 25. *Educational Researcher*, 32(1), 25–28.

Streibel, M. J. (1991). Instructional design and human practice: What can we learn from Grundy's interpretation of Habermas' theory of technical and practical human interests? In R. Muffoletto & N. N. Knupfer (Eds.), *Computers in education: Social, political and historical perspectives* (pp. 141–162). Cresskill, NJ: Hampton.

Stubbs, S. T. (2006). *Design drawing in instructional design at Brigham Young University's Center for Instructional Design: A case study*. (PhD dissertation), Brigham Young University, Salt Lake City, UT.

Stubbs, S. T., & Gibbons, A. S. (2008). The pervasiveness of design drawing in ID. In L. Botturi & T. Stubbs (Eds.), *Handbook of visual languages for instructional design: Theories and practices* (pp. 345–365). Hershey, PA: Information Science Reference.

van Manen, M. (1991). *The tact of teaching: The meaning of pedagogical thoughtfulness.* Albany, NY: SUNY Press.

Warburton, S., & Mor, Y. (2015). A set of patterns for the structured design of MOOCs. *Open Learning: The Journal of Open, Distance and e-Learning,* 30(3), 206–220.

Warburton, S., Mor, Y., & Koskinen, T. (2015). Design patterns for open online teaching and learning (editorial). *eLearning Papers,* 42.

Wittmann, E. (1995). Mathematics education as a 'design science.' *Educational Studies in Mathematics,* 29(4), 355–374.

Yinger, R. J. (1989). *A pattern language for teaching (a planning/working document for the School of Education).* University of Cincinnati, Cincinnati, OH.

Yinger, R. J. (2008). A pattern language (personal corespondence).

Yinger, R. J., & Hendricks-Lee, M. S. (1992). A pattern language for teacher education. *Journal of Teacher Education,* 43, 367–375.

**FIGURE 2.1** The use of pattern in café branding identity creates cohesion across different media

# 2

# INTRODUCING THE PATTERNS

Search online for *principles of design* and you will get millions of results. Without checking more than a handful of these documents, you will find that such terms as pattern, repetition, proximity, contrast, emphasis, balance, scale, harmony, movement, rhythm, unity, and variety appear repeatedly. If you did not know it before you ran that search, you will realize quickly that no single authority offers the definitive list. This list of principles appears on one site and a slightly different list appears on the next site. Browsing through the design section in a library or book store leaves the same impression: no central authority has declared that these principles belong on the authorized list and these other principles do not. That disclaimer about authority notwithstanding, some names—the Getty Museum, for example—will strike you as more authoritative than others. And their lists may therefore be somewhat more persuasive than some others. Still, ultimately, all such lists are simply part of what we might call the design conversation, a conversation that has been going on in print for at least two millennia, and likely longer. Ultimately, any such list is necessarily a selection from among the hundreds of possible principles that a more exhaustive list might include (two examples being Alexander et al., 1977; Ching, 1979).

The conversation about design principles shapes the approach I offer to course and unit planning in this book. I distinguish between the concepts of *planning* and *design*: I view *planning* as the process of deciding what I and my students will do in each lesson, unit, or course, and *design* as the application of design principles to the planning process to ensure that the curriculum and instructional plans I make are simple and elegant. I want simple and elegant plans because students become more powerful learners when they understand how and where a given lesson fits into its unit and how that unit fits into their course.

**FIGURE 2.2** Towers in a financial district are first designed, then built

Chapters 3 to 12 present a selection of just ten design principles, which in this book I often call *patterns*. Although intentionally implementing any one of these patterns would likely produce improvements in students' understanding of the material in a particular course or unit, the patterns I present in these chapters work singly but they work best in concert, as a pattern language (Alexander, 1979, pp. 126–127.). The educator who brings all these principles to bear in his or her design of a course or unit will witness a multiplier effect in student learning. For example, in Chapter 5 ('Entrances and Exits') I argue that educators need to begin new units or themes with clear and inviting entrances. Students need to know they have begun a new section of the course. And they need to know—that is, we need to mark clearly—when units and topics end. Implementing the pattern of entrances and exits by itself would increase students' learning power and improve their learning experience, especially those weaker students for whom course demarcations are sometimes fuzzy. However well any single pattern might work on its own, when combined into a language, the ten connected patterns become more powerful.

## Centres: Chapter 3

The list of ten patterns begins (in Chapter 3) with centres. So many teacher-training programs have adopted the concept of *the big idea* from the work of Jay McTighe and Grant Wiggins that this phrase now has a natural home in the

**FIGURE 2.3** Centres focus the attention of a viewer of an artwork and enable students to recognize quickly the main point of a lesson or unit

educational lexicon (McTighe & Wiggins, 1999, 2005, 2013). And rightly so, for students have a right to know the main point of what they are learning; they are able to organize their thinking and thereby increase the depth of their learning when they know where their teacher means to take them. I start with the centre not only because so many educators know and speak this language but because this is arguably the most important of the principles I will present. The other patterns, in a sense, organize themselves around this pattern.

McTighe and Wiggins understand the big idea as just that: an idea. I argue that a centre could also be a culminating activity or major assessment. So, for example, in the language of McTighe and Wiggins, the big idea in a science unit might be that the water cycle works in a certain way. That understanding of a centre fits completely with my understanding inasmuch as a teacher might teach the water cycle with the main purpose of having students understand how the water cycle works. But the big idea fits with my concept of a centre only as an example and not as a synonym. As I use the term in this book, the centre of the unit—*the main thing* in the unit—might be a trip to a local river, or it might be a major project related to the water cycle. On my account, ideas count, but the centre of a unit might be something other than an idea.

## Boundaries: Chapter 4

In "The Mending Wall," Robert Frost claims that there is something "that doesn't love a wall" (1979). A century of continued efforts to move toward integrated curriculum may bear out the truth of his claim in educational circles (Badley, 2009). But the failure to implement integrated curriculum in most settings may indicate that Frost was not thinking about education when he wrote those words. Granted, he also concedes that in some situations good fences make

**FIGURE 2.4** Boundaries such as fences and roads separate the parts of towns and buildings. Boundaries help students to know what belongs in a lesson and what does not

good neighbours and, as I argue in Chapter 4, when it comes to design of instruction, it is both possible and necessary to make "good fences." We and our students need clear demarcations between what fits and what does not fit in a given course or unit. We need to be able to tell a student that, yes, that project suits the learning outcomes of the unit we are in at this time. And we need to be able to say that, no, that other idea actually does not belong here, but it does connect to a unit we will be working on two months from now or even to a unit that the student will encounter two years from now.

We demarcate property edges and fields with roads, fences, walls, hedges, rows of trees. Towns and cities use zoning laws as a means of demarcation, and they divide neighbourhoods with arterial roads, transition zones, parks, and other public spaces. This is all done to isolate residential areas from traffic or industrial noise or to keep those who sell certain products at a reasonable distance from schools. Inside buildings, we use walls, baffles, planters, furniture, and even variations in flooring material to mark boundaries and edges. Prominent among the reasons we do so is that boundaries and edges help focus attention on the centre. Linguistics may offer another reason: that we need to categorize and name the world in which we find ourselves because an unclassified world would make us crazy. Hayakawa's landmark essay, "On Classification" (1964), explores this human need to impose order, as perhaps does Bob Dylan's song, "Man Gave Names to All the Animals." For whatever combination of reasons, we divide things up and separate them from each other.

Educators accept as a given that because school years run as long as they do, we need to break the program of studies in each subject area into smaller parts. In this book, I refer to those smaller parts as units, a term that some equate with theme or topic. Even at the university level some distinguish units, perhaps calling them blocks or sections. Units have advantages besides breaking up a long year into shorter parts. With the subject matter divided, and with the divisions' boundaries clear and scheduled (to whatever specific degree), students can grasp more easily the parameters of their current topics of study in relation to what topics yet lie ahead. Chapter 10's discussion of scale relates to this question; units are one means of reducing the apparent mass of a year's work in a subject area to manageable portions. Boundaries help students define those portions.

Units accomplish the same thing for teachers. Teachers need to plan a year's instruction, and units seem like a natural way to divide the months of the school year into manageable parts. This is not the venue to recount the history of the instructional unit. It is sufficient to note here that most K-12 educators today take for granted that courses are divided into units. Units serve our students in important ways, and we find them indispensable ourselves. Well-designed units have well-demarcated boundaries and Chapter 4 focuses on those boundaries, as well as the kinds of boundary activities that help students connect the unit they are in to the whole course and to their lives outside school.

## Entrances and Exits: Chapter 5

If the school year is to be divided up into sections called units, and those units are to be separated from each other by boundaries, then they must also include entrances so that students can move through or across the boundaries. In Chapter 5, I argue that the first day of a course or unit should function like the entrance and foyer in a building. Grand entrances and foyers announce that one has entered an important or special place. Time spent introducing a course or unit is not wasted if students come to understand that they have begun something life-giving and rich. Short of that, they need to understand that they have begun a topic different from the one they were studying a few days earlier.

**FIGURE 2.5** We need ways in and out of places and spaces we use

Students also need to know when a section of their school year, a unit, ends. Educational researchers have agreed that classes that end intentionally—that are *closed*—result in more learning than classes that simply drift toward a bell (Bloomquist, 2010). Similarly, I argue that units also need to end intentionally, and not simply drift toward a Friday. To return to the architectural metaphor, units need exits; students should know when the current unit of study is going to end and that it will end with something important, whether that is an assessment, an exposition, a day for poster displays or presentations, or some other culminating activity.

## Coherence and Connection: Chapter 6

Chapter 6 explores a challenge faced by designers, architects, and, to the point of this book, educators: demonstrating that the parts fit the whole. Different designers and architects express this pattern in different ways, one of which is reflected in the chapter's title, "Coherence and Connection." Some demand that the building fit in its context or that all the buildings connect to the street, and the internal parts of the building must connect to each other and to the exterior. Others speak of the parts needing to connect to the whole. Christopher Alexander calls for complementarity rather than isolation. Many expressions, same idea.

Applied to curriculum design, this metaphor means that the course must fit into the curriculum and the unit, in turn, must belong and be seen to belong in the course. Individual lessons, too, must suit the unit of which they are part. Whether we scale this principle up or down, the demand holds constant: the parts must fit the whole. Where does that leave us as educators? Architects use windows, doors, cladding, alcoves, benches, and courtyards to connect a building to its context. They quote from and echo nearby buildings to demonstrate that their building fits. Educators must use parallel devices such as reminding students

**FIGURE 2.6** The parts must connect to the whole

of content links to other course sections or pointing to connections between a content area and an overall course objective. Students should never have to wonder how what they are learning fits into the larger picture.

I argue in Chapter 6 that, where possible, professors and teachers should think of the whole course as a street and should develop a short phrase that becomes the street name for the course, for example: "Ideologies in conflict" for 20th-century history. Thinking of the course as a street and the parts of the course as buildings will help remind both teachers and students to identify the links between part and whole.

## Green Spaces: Chapter 7

Everyone should have access to green space. In city centres, these spaces might be as small as pocket-parks, but most residential areas have access to larger playgrounds and parks. In residential areas developed in the last few decades, green spaces might include networks of bike and walking paths built separately and well away from the arterial roads used by motor traffic. Of course, private green spaces include residential backyards and courtyards, and, on a smaller scale, balconies with potted plants.

Students understand that they and their instructors must meet course objectives and that doing so will require pushing ahead and doing hard work. Still, neither students nor teachers can push all the time without becoming bored and fatigued. So, I argue in Chapter 7 that courses, units, and individual classes must include quiet spaces with easier content, such as the inclusion of narrative passages in a course that mostly uses expository text, or a presentation by a guest speaker in any course. Teachers and professors can use video in a lecture-based course, and if they do so carefully and intentionally, offering students adequate scaffolding, they can do so unapologetically. As Neil Postman reminded us decades ago

**FIGURE 2.7** Students and teachers need places to breathe

(1985), screens pull the eyes, and teachers who use screens carefully can bring instructional content to students while having students think they are getting a break from instruction.

At the micro-scale, individual class sessions can include small but restorative green spaces. Even the KWL (what I **K**now, what I **W**ould like to know, what I **L**earned) sheet or one of its many adaptations (such as TLW: **T**hink, **L**earned, **W**onder) can provide a break from other modes of instruction. Likewise, Think-Pair-Share, used carefully, can function as a break, as can many other quick strategies known to most K–12 teachers.

## Public and Private: Chapter 8

In cities, towns, public buildings, and private homes, everyone needs spaces that they can call their own. People also need public spaces in which they can gather together. City planners and architects have struggled with this public-private tension for over two thousand years. If we accept Charles Taylor's argument that the contemporary concept of the self or the individual came about relatively recently, we then have to recognize that the demand for privacy actually preceded the invention of selfhood as we understand it (Taylor, 1987).

In Chapter 8, I work with the public-private question metaphorically to distinguish the modes in which our students work. I note that much of our instruction and assessment is common to all the students in a class: they complete the same readings, they do the same assignments, they participate in common class activities, and they receive common instruction. In the metaphor's terms, these common activities are public. Indeed, educational funding demands that we conduct our classes in this way. However, in light of how much of our students' experience is common to all, courses, units, lessons, physical classrooms, and instructional time should also be organized so that students find times and

**FIGURE 2.8** Students need a place of their own

places where they can work alone and where assessment is based solely on work they complete alone. We should plan student assessment so that students have plentiful opportunities to choose their own work, as long as their work suits the course and unit objectives.

Most educators would likely agree that curriculum and instructional planning have what I call the public mode as their default setting. I do not protest public features of curriculum and instruction, such as direct instruction, class discussions, class presentations, debates, and reading aloud. In fact, depending on the materials and grade level, curriculum designers and instructors should direct a portion of the course assessment toward public work. But I argue in Chapter 8 that we should also be more intentional about the public aspects of our instruction, so that whole-class activities become much more than the default mode of teaching and learning and rather that they almost become venues of civic celebration and sources of civic, classroom energy.

## Variety, Repetition, and Contrast: Chapter 9

At the opening of this chapter, I suggested searching online for *principles of design*. I noted there both that such a search would yield millions of records and that the lists of design principles vary. However, the ideas I treat in Chapter 9 of this book nearly always appear on such lists. So, how does one combine these elements to create a work of art, or a building, or a city? Buildings and towns need both variety and repetition. Endless repetition, for all the efficiencies it offers, induces boredom, in both physical and pedagogical environments. Artists and designers view variety and contrast as ways to balance repetition, not as contradictions of it.

In the classroom, teacher and students alike need a free and ordered place, to gloss a book title from some decades ago (Giamatti, 1988). At the same time,

**FIGURE 2.9** Combine repetition and variety

nearly universally, students find courses boring where the teacher does the same thing every day, in other words, where there is too much order. Of course, there are exceptions to that generalization. If the wisest person on earth and the funniest person on earth co-taught a course, they could probably use direct instruction for 90 minutes every day for a whole semester and never face a complaint. But mere mortals like us who are less funny or less wise need to vary our teaching methods.

On the other hand, students need repetition. Familiar instructional methods and modes of content allow them to concentrate on the subject matter. Familiar assignments and rubrics free them to focus on the content of their work rather than on grading schemas. The claim that variety is the spice of life might not have originated in a classroom, but it certainly applies to classrooms. The saying's cliché status perhaps leads us to miss something important: variety is not the main course of life. If school were characterized only by endless variety, students' heads would spin, and their education would be harmed.

In Chapter 9, I examine variety and repetition, suggesting ways that both can enhance learning, and calling for the kinds of contrast that enhance students' sense of coherence and unity.

## Gradients, Harmony and Scale: Chapter 10

Designers, architects, town planners, and educators all must confront issues related to scale. How does one make a small room look bigger? How does one make a large room or building look more accessible and approachable? And how does one make a massive and difficult course look manageable, so students do not give up in despair when they first glance at the syllabus? These are questions of scale. They connect to gradients and harmony inasmuch as variations in scale can bring a sense of harmony to a building or a course. In instructional settings,

FIGURE 2.10 Combine a range of sizes with human scale

offering instructional sections (units) in a balanced range of sizes can help students view the more difficult and massive sections as exceptional and therefore more manageable.

In Chapter 10, I take up these issues in earnest, applying to curriculum and instruction some of the strategies architects use to reduce the appearance of mass—the intimidation—that such buildings often induce from the street. Some designers prefer to set the building back from the property line, thus offering the public a small plaza or park. Early in the history of skyscrapers, architects in Chicago and New York began to use another kind of setback, designing the tower of the building with a smaller footprint than the four or five bottom stories. This type of setback changes the view of the building for the person standing beneath it on the sidewalk; its mass is reduced and, as a whole, it becomes less intimidating. In this chapter I argue that the introduction to the course or unit should build the student's confidence, not intimidate the student or make the student feel stupid and incapable. And I will note that the most difficult component of a course should be scaffolded and introduced over a couple class periods to reduce intimidation.

## Master Planning, Piecemeal Development, Roughness: Chapter 11

Whether you are a pre-service teacher or a veteran educator, you know that pedagogical Rome was not built in a day. Like people learning to skate or snowboard, educators fall and get up, and fall and get up. After four or five iterations, a course starts to get good; both we and our students like it. Likewise, after several cohorts of students have used a teaching-learning strategy that we have devised or adapted, we finally figure out its optimal structure. We know what materials we need to have on hand in advance. We finally get the

**FIGURE 2.11** Organic growth is superior to master planning

instructions worded correctly so that almost everyone can understand them. And we know how many minutes it takes for a class to use the activity.

Contrast this story of piecemeal development with the mental posture that often lies behind master planning. A process of master planning might yield what those involved consider a perfect curriculum: the students will study this, then they will move on to this, and finally they will know this. The difficulty with this approach to planning is that it ignores our own weaknesses as educators and the near-complete unpredictability of student responses to the material and approaches we bring them. Yet, those who swear by master planning often approach the implementation of a plan as if it will encounter no bumps.

In Chapter 11, I argue not only that there will be bumps and that we need to plan for them, but that the bumps and our responses to them actually enrich curriculum and instruction. Like old streets and old buildings that we feel at home in because they show the rich wear and tear of long human use, our units and lessons should show the rich results of previous students' responses to our designs. We should tell our students quite frankly what the unit looked like before, some of the things that did not go so well, and how we adapted the materials and learning strategies in response. In other words, we should reveal our work. The principles in this chapter are firmly planted on the ground of learning from our teaching mistakes, of listening to our students' complaints, and of getting it right eventually.

## Agile, Light Structures: Chapter 12

In ordinary circumstances, bridge designers must deal with three kinds of loads: dead loads (the weight of the bridge itself), live loads (traffic, snow), and wind. One way or another, the first two kinds of load must be transferred to the ground. Simple, sparse bridge designs can handle the required loads and still look

**FIGURE 2.12** Simple, elegant designs can handle classroom forces

elegant, even beautiful. I work with bridge metaphors in Chapter 12 to argue that simple, elegant instructional designs increase students' sense of self-efficacy, and thereby the depth and quality of their learning, by offering them clear and simple ways to scaffold and organize the curriculum materials.

Some bridge designers gain the reputations they do because of the ways they combine engineering and art into strong, elegant forms, such as Robert Maillart's Salginatobel Bridge in the Swiss canton of Graubunden *or* Ben van Berkel's Erasmus Bridge in Rotterdam. Viewers of such bridges proclaim them brilliant, or beautiful, or both. Chapter 12 asks us to take the best ideas from some of these designers' bridges and build unit structures as light and elegant as theirs. Just as bridges must withstand three types of loads, teachers, students, and classes must withstand pedagogical and administrative loads. I argue in Chapter 12 that simple, elegant structures can withstand the characteristic loads of classroom work better than clunky structures can.

## Building a Unit or Theme: Chapter 13

In Chapters 13 and 14, I show two different ways that patterns work together. Although this book as a whole is not a how-to, I devote Chapter 13 to a step-by-step explanation of how to plan a single unit of several weeks' duration using the pattern language that I have placed on offer. I combine the principles from Chapters 3 through 12 to show how this pattern language lands on the actual ground of instructional planning. Over the two years during which I wrote this book, I worked with approximately 125 K-12 teachers and 15 professors to refine the steps and clarify the instructions I offer here. Late in Chapter 13, I argue that our contemporary work circumstances demand that our planning processes be agile; we must be able to adapt patterns and implement new ideas mid-course or mid-unit, and on the fly. At the end of the chapter, I suggest that

**FIGURE 2.13** Planning a unit using the patterns in Chapters 3 to 12

we plan big changes, that we develop a three-to-five year plan for making substantial revisions to our instructional program in light of the pattern language I offer in this volume, and that we do so on a human and humane schedule.

## Conclusion: Chapter 14

Chapter 14 begins with a brief treatment of the concept of scalability. The book focuses on how patterns apply in the design of units or topics, but patterns can also be scaled down to individual lessons and up to whole courses or even to an entire curriculum. Educators today face more pressures than educators in earlier decades or centuries faced. They need approaches to their work that can easily be scaled up and down. The ten principles I describe in this book possess the scalability that educators need.

The second part of Chapter 14 circles back to some of the questions I raised in Chapter 1, especially the question of how well an aesthetic approach to planning such as I offer here fits with the dominant planning models currently on offer in most education programs and practiced by most K-12 teachers and many in higher education.

In Chapter 1 and again in the first paragraphs of this chapter, I noted that many others before me have suggested pattern languages. This was true first in architecture, and in fact the phrase *pattern language* was coined by architect Christopher Alexander. In the 1990s, the software community took up Alexander's ideas and worked at developing a pattern language for software development. Late in that same decade and into the new millennium, educators began to take seriously the possibility that pattern language could be an efficient way to share pedagogical knowledge. Computer science educators were the first to talk about pattern languages for teaching. The conversation spread to online instruction in general and then to educators in all fields and at all levels.

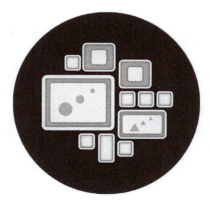

**FIGURE 2.14** Patterns can be scaled up or down

In this book, I do not devote many pages either to the theory underlying pattern languages or to a history of the adoption and uses of pattern languages in education, but I do wish to provide those readers who want to read more with some suggestions. Such suggestions appear throughout the book. I owe thanks to Christopher Alexander and to many others. At this point, I wish simply to re-iterate that my biggest design-theory debt is to Alexander. The bibliography of works by him and, in some cases, by him and various colleagues, runs to several pages. The main Alexandrian influences behind this project are these: *A Pattern Language*, with its more than 200 patterns (1977), *The Timeless Way of Building* (1979), *The Oregon Experiment* (1975), and volumes 1 to 4 of *A Vision of The Living World*, which many readers have viewed as more of a work in aesthetic philosophy than a work in design *per sé* (2005).

## References

Alexander, C. (1979). *The timeless way of building*. New York: Oxford University Press.

Alexander, C. (2005*). A vision of the living world: The nature of order* (volume 3). Berkeley, CA: The Center for Environmental Structure.

Alexander, C., Ishikawa, S., Silverstein, M., Jacobson, M., Fiksdahl-King, I., & Angel, S. (1977). *A pattern language: Towns, buildings, construction*. New York: Oxford University Press.

Alexander, C., Silverstein, M., Angel, S., Ishikawa, S., & Abrams, D. (1975). *The Oregon experiment*. New York: Oxford University Press.

Badley, K. (2009). Resistance to curriculum integration: Do good fences make good neighbors? *Issues in Integrative Studies*, 27, 113–127. Retrieved from https://our.oakland.edu/handle/10323/14450.

Bloomquist, T. (2010). *Effectiveness of closure in lesson design: A quasi-experimental investigation*. (EdD dissertation). Newberg, OR: George Fox University.

Ching, F. D. K. (1979). *Architecture, form, space & order*. Reinhold: Van Nostrand.

Frost, R. (1979). *The poetry of Robert Frost: The collected poems, complete and unabridged*. New York: Holt.

Giamatti, A. B. (1988). *A free and ordered space: The real world of the university*. New York: Norton.

Hayakawa, S. I. (1964). *Language in thought and action*. New York: Harcourt, Brace & World.

McTighe, J., & Wiggins, G. (1999). *Understanding by design handbook*. Alexandria, VA: Association for Supervision and Curriculum Development.

McTighe, J., & Wiggins, G. (2005). *Understanding by design* (2nd ed.). Alexandria, VA: Association for Supervision and Curriculum Development.

McTighe, J., & Wiggins, G. (2013). *Essential questions: Opening doors to student understanding*. Alexandria, VA: ACSD.

Postman, N. (1985). *Amusing ourselves to death: Public discourse in the age of show business*. New York: Viking.

Taylor, C. (1987). *Sources of the self: The making of the modern identity*. Boston, MA: Harvard University Press.

**FIGURE 3.1** City plan and map both draw viewer's eyes to the centre of Paris

# 3
# STRONG CENTRES

Students sometimes ask their teachers, "What's the point of this?" The particular word, *point*, has two possible meanings in that question, "what is the main idea here?" and "why are we doing this?" In the mouths of some students, the why question has an implied and somewhat biting extension, "Why are we even in school?" In those moments when students ask what the point is, as in life, the two meanings may be connected. If students know the main idea—the point— they are supposed to be learning in a given bit of instruction, they may be less inclined to ask about the purpose—the point—of why they are in class at that moment.

Using the design concept of centres, this chapter discusses the point. Many educators now start their planning by identifying *the big idea*. Typing *lesson planning the big idea* into a search bar yielded 2,700,000 records just now. Aside from the fact that search bars did not exist when I received my initial teaching certificate, I do not recall that many educators were using that language at that time (although Bloom's taxonomy was in its heyday at the time). Likewise, the phrases *learning outcomes* and *backwards by design* were not in the language then. If *essential questions*, *rich questions*, and *fertile questions* were in the lexicon, they were certainly not in common use. Presumably, educators aimed at something, but they used different language to describe their targets.

Centuries before these phrases made their appearance in the educational lexicon, artists and designers were already discussing centres. In the oldest surviving treatise on architecture, *The Ten Books on Architecture* (*de architectura*, in Latin, written between 30 and 15 BC), a Roman engineer named Marcus Vitruvius Pollio treated centres. Indeed, they are an old concern. In this chapter, I work back and forth between the pedagogical challenge of the big idea and the design concept of the centre. As I do in several of the chapters that follow,

I begin the chapter by discussing a teaching challenge in its context. I then explore a similar challenge in the world of architecture or design, following that with some of the solutions that architects and designers have devised. I then move the discussion back to education, making applications of the design solutions to the world of classrooms.

## A Teaching Challenge in its Context

One of the first challenges we face as educators as we prepare for instruction is to make clear what the main thing is we want our students to learn. What is the main idea that runs through the lesson, the unit, or, for that matter, the course? What are the areas of focus and weight? What ideas are more important than others. If this course were a Greek building, what would be the columns that support the roof? The water cycle has these main features; valence is an important property of elements because of this; the French revolution was a response to these pressures; we are willing to suspend our disbelief when we attend the theatre for these reasons. These are big ideas.

Almost every teacher entering service today already knows this truth, in large part because of the popularity of the idea of *backwards by design* and the work of Jay McTighe and Grant Wiggins (McTighe & Wiggins, 1999, 2005, 2013). I noted in Chapter 1 that readers should not read my book as a critique of their work and that my overall concern in the book is to address a quite separate question from the one they ask. However, their work accords perfectly with my purpose of this chapter, that we must be clear with ourselves and our students regarding what we want them to learn. Richard Dufour asked teachers to ask themselves what their students really needed to know, and then to select ruthlessly what to teach (2010). With him and with McTighe and Wiggins, we all need to ask what is the organizing idea or central concept of the instruction we are asking our students to be part of?

McTighe and Wiggins ask us to focus on the big issues. In backwards by design, we identify the desired outcomes (or, typically, have them identified for us), we identify what assessment evidence would assure us that our students have learned what we meant them to learn, and then we work backwards to identify what are the needed steps—what learning plan—we need to follow to get to those results. Viewed from one direction, nothing makes more sense. My students tell me regularly about a class in my university where, day after day, the professor shows a deck of PowerPoint slides provided to him by the publisher of the course textbook. Students take notes from these slides and they write a mid-term exam and a final exam, provided by the publisher, based on the information on these slides. I want to trust that the instructor in question periodically thinks about the big ideas that are supposed to drive that course.

Unironically, I suspect, this professor has also mounted all the course material on the course web-site and has welcomed students not to attend class if they would prefer to study the course materials by viewing the PowerPoint slides online. My guess is that this professor pushes the Page Down button about 75 times in 75 minutes and earns a lot of money for doing so, perhaps proving the truth of the adage that power corrupts and PowerPoint corrupts absolutely. Another saying, the origins of which we will likely never establish but which surely applies to this professor, runs that if you can be replaced by a computer you should be. My point here is that someone earning minimum wage could push the *Page Down* button as skilfully as this professor does and could transmit the knowledge on those slides nearly as skilfully as he transmits that knowledge. Well, not quite. He likely answers a question from time to time that would stump our minimum-wage worker (although my students have told me he does not really warm to questions). Replace every professor who "teaches" mainly by pushing a *Page Down* key and the university's budget crunch would be solved.

Back to McTighe and Wiggins for a moment, if this professor and others like him would, in a sense, start their courses by asking about their desired learning outcomes instead of by asking how many PowerPoint decks the textbook publisher provided—in other words, if they tried what we now call *backwards by design*—their classes might be more transformative for their students. But I have peeked through enough classroom windows to know that this change is not coming tomorrow. Still, the sad state of affairs, at least in higher education, underlines the importance of what McTighe and Wiggins have called for.

The question of centres and big ideas holds in inquiry learning as well. Inquiry obviously ranges across a continuum from teacher-driven to student-driven. Teacher-driven inquiry starts something like this: "these are the big questions that you will need to research on this topic. So, develop hypotheses about these questions, find ways to research and test your hypotheses, and draw conclusions." In its strongest form, student-driven inquiry starts more along these lines: "you need to identify the big questions that you think are raised by what we have looked at. Then, you will need to develop hypotheses . . ." and so on. Some proponents of inquiry will quibble over my inclusion of the teacher-driven example above, but because agreeing on a definition of inquiry that satisfies all educational stakeholders is impossible, I will not give more attention to that question here.

Educators and students alike should be thankful for McTighe and Wiggins and the many others who have reminded us all that instruction needs a point and that students need to know what that point is. As I noted, designers and architects have worked with this question for centuries, and we turn now to their handling of the same problem.

## A Parallel Problem in Design

Artists and designers face the same challenge that educators face. They want the eyes of those who view a work to be drawn immediately to a centre. Architects and city planners want those who enter a space to be able to identify immediately the centre of that space. City planners even devise ways to protect central spaces. Through the use of narrowed streets, pedestrian-only zones, traffic signals, congestion fees, and cobbled pavements, planners sometimes route vehicle traffic away from and pedestrian traffic toward a central square or plaza. Cities draw life from their centres and planners see it as their mandate to protect those centres and to make them easy to find.

Because of their concern that the rest of us find the centre, designers, artists, city planners, and architects all strive to avoid extraneous elements. Figure 3.2 illustrates a failure to show viewers a centre. Three colours of stucco combine with two other kinds of cladding and the faux timbers supporting the entry roof on these townhouses to leave viewers wondering what they are expected to look at. Useless adornments and extra features abound in these townhouses, like a bad writer's expository essay that wanders in the wild spaces but never makes a point.

One small feature of these townhouses (showing in Figure 3.3) warrants further comment. A wrist-sized, plastic pipe draining the roof over the front entry actually directs water onto the path of anyone approaching the front door. I do not want to push the metaphor so far that it collapses, but this feature illustrates a point about extraneous elements: we call them extraneous because they are not needed; they distract from the work. As it turns out, not only can

**FIGURE 3.2**
Near the author's home, new town houses lack a central theme. Five kinds of cladding reduce coherence

**FIGURE 3.3**
Confused design results in a stalagmite-producing roof drain placed over a front step

**FIGURE 3.4** Sweeping waves of steel at the Edmonton Art Gallery

they distract, they can detract and diminish, even do harm. In this case, fortunately, the metre-high icicle produced by spring melt-water dripping from the drain cannot fall on anyone's head. Were it a stalactite rather than a stalagmite, the homeowner might want to worry.

The tight-budget townhouses in Figures 3.2 and 3.3 are not alone in having failed to make the centre clear. Iconic public buildings sometimes suffer from the same problem, as illustrated by the art gallery in Figure 3.4. The Edmonton Art Gallery's stainless waves have the potential to brighten a winter morning, but one's eyes are not drawn toward either a centre or an entrance (Chapter 5).

Having mentioned unclear writing with reference to the townhouses in Figures 3.2 and 3.3, I will return to matters of writing briefly as another example of a problem in design. Many of my readers will have taught writing and will have accompanied students in their struggle to understand the simple concept of the thesis statement (at least composition teachers consider it simple). To us, the differences between "The French revolution went wrong for these four reasons," and "This paper is about the French revolution," are absolutely clear; the first is a thesis statement, the second is an announcement. But some students literally cannot detect the difference between the two sentences. To my point, the paper following their opening paragraph will betray their failure to identify their main point. If we offer wise advice along the lines of "The thesis is to the paper as the plot is to the novel," a few students might then understand, but not all. Stepping it up with "The thesis is to the paper as the locomotive is to the train" might

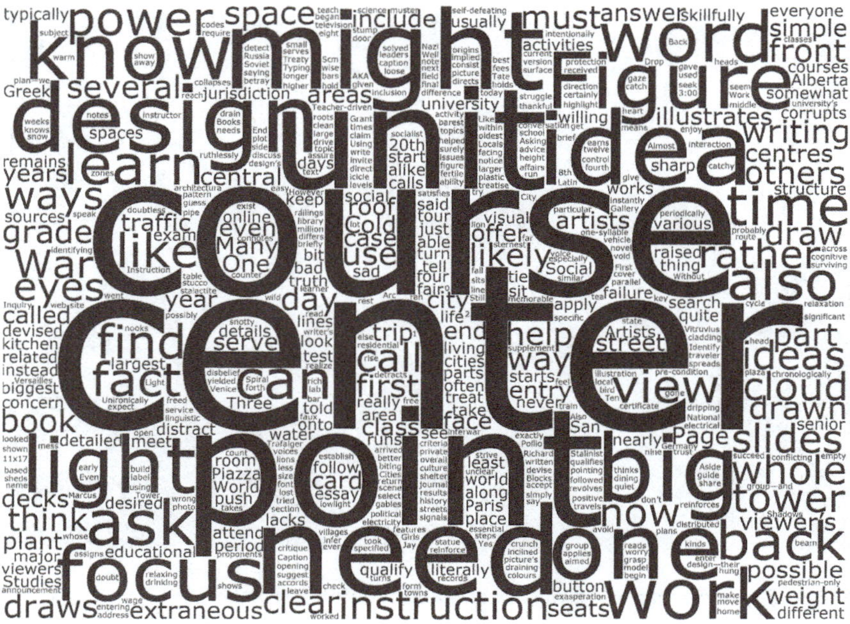

**FIGURE 3.5** Viewers of word clouds do not know what to focus on or what connections exist between the words

help a few more. Asking, in exasperation, "What's your point?" might help a few more. The example, while from writing, not from design, sheds more light on the question of the need for an obvious centre.

Most readers will have had a student submit a word cloud as part of an assignment. Arguably, because an online word cloud generator preserves the largest font size for those words that appear most often in the submitted text, the word cloud may serve some purpose as a supplement to an assignment. Also, arguably, the viewer's eyes may be drawn to the largest words in the word cloud, thereby meeting the criteria for a centre. But, in honesty, the word cloud is a graphic mess, and if one argues that the viewer's eyes are drawn to a centre, then one must concede that that centre is more a linguistic or cognitive centre than a graphic centre.

## Solutions to Design Problems

Planners, architects, artists, and designers have developed ways to help us find and focus on the centre. For example, the AKA business card shown in Figure 3.6 instantly draws the viewer's eyes to the main point. We know that we will need to turn the card over to find the contact information or to learn what The Design Girls might be willing to design for us. But the front of the card draws much of its power from its visual centre, and it draws us. That power to draw also roots itself in the design's simplicity and clean structure, topics which I treat in Chapter 12.

The fountain in Figure 3.7 functions as a centre in two or maybe three ways. First, it is the visual centre of the photograph, composed intentionally by the photographer to achieve a certain result. Second, because it dominates the composition, our eyes are drawn to it. But it is literally the centre of the garden as well, as the cement tiles and borders of the patio make clear. Only after looking for a few moments, do we notice other plants, the windows, or the grape vines suspended above. The photographer, a secondary teacher, did not have this book in mind when he took this photograph. But he had the principle of centres very much in mind, and his photograph illustrates the principle well.

As does the fountain (Figure 3.7), the CN Tower in Toronto (Figure 3.8) also functions as the centre of an image. This poster illustrates how artists use positive and negative space (background) to help viewers find and focus on the subject. When viewing this poster, one's eyes are drawn immediately to the tower. The empty background is, in a sense, nothing; it is the void, but it functions importantly in this picture by pushing us to notice the tower. It reinforces rather than detracts from the picture's centre. The tower in the graphic is not located in the centre of the poster, but it functions as the centre. Educators

**FIGURE 3.6** The business card for a design firm draws the viewer's eyes instantly to the message of the card. With its simplicity and power, it speaks to the design abilities of The Design Girls

## A DESIGNER'S THOUGHTS ON CENTRES

How do we determine centres? What goes into making that choice? Perhaps in education the mandate is handed down, but in the design world that choice is made by the designer, the architect, or the planner. And sometimes that choice might surprise you. The visual centre of a house might be the entryway but the emotional centre the kitchen, the intellectual centre the study; or the spiritual centre the garden (Figure 3.7). All are centres, or it might be better to say that all **can** be centres; what makes them centres are the people. The architect who designs a chef's house with the centre being the study, is doing their client a disservice. Likewise, the designer who focuses a store's website on something other than the products. This is where a term from usability and digital design hits the nail on the head: user-centred design.

A home's centre is based on who lives there and a website reflects the needs of the business and users. In user-centred design, we work with two questions: what do our users want? what do we want our users to do? One question gives us what the people using our product will see as the centre of the product, service, city, or home, the other gives us what we want them to do along the way. When we tie our goals to what they want, we achieve success. In a simple example, our users want access to the paper we wrote, we want to be able to follow up with them, we ask them for their email in order to send them the paper.

While it may be true to say that there are different types of centres in a city, house, or design, or that centres can exist for different reasons and can exist simultaneously while fulfilling different needs, the question remains: how do you create centres? In design, we create centres using other design principles. This is where you realize that while Chapters 3–12 in this book are sequenced here, they are equally important. Centres come first because they allow the other principles to cohere in pursuit of a single purpose, but they also need to come last, or be revisited, because you need tools to build strong centres.

Aesthetically, a centre is created through contrast, highlighting the centre through a distinct change from its surroundings (Chapter 9: Repetition and Variety, Figure 9.6). Contrast can be achieved through, among other things, colour, size, or typography. Using the principle of movement, designers can use line to create centres, guiding the viewer's eye toward the goal (Chapter 4: Boundaries). Centres can be achieved by setting the subject against white space, or by building white space into a busy design (Chapter 7: Green Spaces). These are just some of the ways designers build centres. We may use one principle or many to achieve our goal, and we match the building blocks to the specific problem of the design, as no solution works for all projects.

Kristen Badley, graphic designer

**FIGURE 3.7** A fountain functions as the centre of a small patio

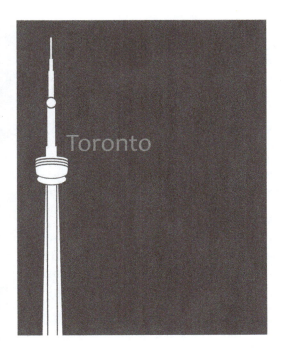

**FIGURE 3.8** The placement of elements in this graphic representation of the CN Tower in Toronto draws the viewer's eyes to the centre

need not think that the centre of a unit must sit chronologically in the middle of the time the unit takes. In a unit on electricity, the trip to the power plant could happen on the second day (especially in an enquiry model); it could be located, so to speak, where the Toronto tower sits in Figure 3.8.

## Solutions in Designing Instruction

Educators at all levels, from Kindergarten through university, have devised ways to meet the challenge of helping students to understand the point, to find the centre. In a workshop where eight teachers and I were planning a science unit called Light and Shadows, I asked, "What is the one thing a student is supposed to know by the end of the unit?" One participant answered immediately, "What is light?" That answer illustrates the idea of a centre perfectly because if the teacher plans the unit so that everything students do connects to that idea; the students will likely learn what they are supposed to. The unit should succeed.

As one might expect, the learning outcomes provided by the jurisdiction run longer than three words. In fact, the main outcome reads that students should be able to "Identify sources of light, describe the interaction of light with different materials, and infer the pathway of a light beam" (Alberta Education, 2015). Even what I quoted above is followed by twelve specific learner expectations related to the sources of light, reflection, shadows, how light travels, and so on. Classroom teachers know about the detailed learning outcomes produced by departments of education. The point made by the workshop participant is that the unit revolves around a centre and that centre can be expressed in three one-syllable words. *What is light?* succinctly catches the purposes of the fourth-grade unit in question. Teacher and students alike will find those words easy to remember.

In the same jurisdiction where fourth-grade students in science still learn about light, high-school seniors in social-studies learned for many years about the 20th century. Their social studies course for that year included seven units, four of them related to political and economic ideologies: *Democracy*, with Sweden, the US and Canada as examples; *Dictatorship*, with Nazi Germany and Stalinist Russia as examples; *Capitalism*, with a focus on Reagan and Thatcher; and *Socialism*, with a focus on Soviet communism and democratic socialist Scandinavia. Three units were meant to cover the history of the 20th century: The Treaty of Versailles, the interwar period and World War 2; the Cold War; the end of the Cold War and the period following, up to whatever year one was teaching the course.

For nine years I taught this sprawling course, the most voluminous course I have ever taught. Half the students' final grades for this course came from assessments in my classroom and half from two exams (of two and a half hours each) administered by the province. In Alberta, teachers and students alike take their diploma exams seriously. With that as background, imagine my surprise when a student asked me why we studied World War II in the course. In part, his question gave rise to this book because it helped me realize that I had not made clear how all the parts connected to the whole (Chapter 6: Coherence and Connections) or, to the point of this chapter, what the whole was. He did not know the point. When I recounted this brief classroom scene to a colleague, she told me to try to summarize the course in two words. *Conflicting ideologies* was the best answer I could offer, and that took several days to produce. Everything in that Alberta grade 12 social studies program connected to that phrase. From that day forward, I distributed an 11 × 17" photocopied graphic meant to look like a street with seven buildings on it. The street name was Conflicting Ideologies and the seven buildings represented the seven units, four (ideologies) on one side of the street and three (historical periods) on the other. With the unwitting help of a student and the intentional help of a colleague, I had found the centre of a massive course.

Equipped with my simple phrase, I found I had better control of the course. I found I could more easily decide what to teach and what to omit. After struggling for some years to keep three of the seven units in check (Democracy, Capitalism, the Cold War and its aftermath), the concept of centres combined with those two words to free me to admit that these three units warranted more time and attention. In fact, I began to tell students that the whole course hung on their understanding the contents of these units, like columns holding up a Greek building. Having allocated more days to those three units, I explained to my students that on the street called Conflicting Ideologies these were the three biggest buildings.

I tell this story at length here to underline the importance of identifying the centre in a unit (or a course). I was not the only beneficiary of this focused perspective. My students' sense of their own control over their learning increased when they knew what the central purpose of the course was and could see how the seven units in this immense course connected to each other. Like Trafalgar Square in London or the Piazza San Marco in Venice, Conflicting Ideologies provided a meeting place; everything in the course connected to that simple idea. At some point, the leaders of a million tour groups have said in the most convincing voice they could muster, "We will meet back here at 3:00; you have to be here by 3:00." In each case, everyone in the group—and, for that matter, nearly everyone in the respective city—would know exactly what and where that meeting point was. Locals might not consider Trafalgar Square to be the centre of London or the Piazza San Marco to be the centre of Venice, but they know how to direct a lost traveler back to that meeting point. That is how the simple phrase, *conflicting ideologies,* functioned in my social studies classroom. That is how centres function.

Several other comments are in order before ending this discussion of centres in the design of curriculum and instruction. First, to follow the principles that designers follow, educators wanting their students to focus on the centre must be willing to design the background intentionally. The townhouses shown in Figure 3.2 had too many distracting features. The Toronto poster in Figure 3.8 had none. Like poster designers, educators must ruthlessly eliminate distracting details and adornments. The background should reinforce rather than detract from the centre. Having identified the centres, we must subdue other elements. The club poster in Figure 3.9 has enough information for young adults to plan an evening out. But visually, it has no centre. It bombards the viewer, perhaps functioning as a metaphor for the kind of evening it advertises. May the club poster never be a metaphor for our courses, units, or lessons. We must eliminate the unimportant to draw our students' focus toward the centre.

Second, we need to remember that larger centres consist of smaller centres, a principle in design generally and a theme among those who work with pattern languages (Alexander, 1979, 2002; Alexander & Mehaffy, 2015; Alexander et al., 1977). The question "What is light?" and the phrase *conflicting ideologies* will tie a unit or a course together, but to keep focused on their day-to-day work, teachers and students will need more detailed scaffolding than is provided by a catchy and memorable two-word phrase or three-word question. We should probably commit ourselves to the discipline of producing two- or three-word

**FIGURE 3.9** A rock poster packed with details but with no visual centre

phrases for all our units and possibly even for our lessons. An instructional place such as a unit will never be as imposing as the Piazza San Marco or Trafalgar Square, but the comparison holds; these famous places consist of many smaller centres. Trafalgar Square has the steps of the National Gallery, Nelson's column, two fountains, The Church of St. Martin-in-the-Fields, and so on, several places to which a tour guide might say, "Be back here at 3:00 sharp." In 2005, a teacher colleague and I mustered our sternest voices and said those very words to a group of high-school students in Trafalgar Square. We were standing in front of one of the lions that protect Nelson's statue. Everyone arrived in front of that lion by 3:00 sharp; no one confused it for the Tate Modern on the other side of the Thames. That is how centres work.

Third, although a program of studies may include 4 units in grade 5 science, or six units in tenth-grade mathematics, we do not need to allocate the same amount of time to each of them in our course design. In Chapter 9 (Repetition and Variety) and Chapter 10 (Gradients, Harmony, and Levels of Scale), I will argue that all units do not need to be—in fact, should not be—the same size. As I noted in my recounting of my experience with senior social studies, we should identify the most important units, the ones that hold up the course like the columns in a Greek or Roman building.

Fourth, we should remember Jerome Bruner's concept of the spiral curriculum (1960). He encouraged educators to come back around to topics repeatedly, each time asking our students to explore those topics with new questions and new perspectives. One participant in the contemporary conversation about patterns calls the spiral a pattern (Bergin, 2000, Pattern #32). Bergin argues the necessity of returning repeatedly to fragments so that students can understand the whole.

## Conclusion

Finally, we must remember that our own perspective on centres likely differs from our students' perceptions. We may view the fair where students present their hand-built electrical devices as the centre of the unit. In our view, the fair was always the end point of the research and much of the instruction. Some students will share our view. But others will doubtless think of the trip to the power plant as the highlight of the unit, possibly of the whole year. For *trip to the power plant*, substitute the phrase *unit test* and ask how many students will think of that as the centre of the unit. We are making a mistake if we view a major assessment as the centre when our students will consider it the lowlight of the unit.

In the mid-chapter textbox titled "A Designer's Thoughts on Centres," the web-site designer who designed much of this book pointed out that user experience—what she calls UX—is central to effective web-site design. In fact, she often answers the "What do you do?" question with "I'm a UX specialist." If we want our students to know what the light unit is about, or why World

War II is in a course, we may want to become UX specialists ourselves. Once we view ourselves that way, we may recognize that one of our first tasks is to design courses, units, and lessons so that our students can easily find the centre.

## References

Alberta Education. (2015). *Program of studies, science*: Retrieved from https://education.alberta.ca/science-k-6/program-of-studies/everyone/programs-of-study/.

Alexander, C. (1979). *The timeless way of building*. New York: Oxford University Press.

Alexander, C. (2002). *The phenomenon of life: The nature of order* (volume 1). Berkeley, CA: The Centre for Environmental Structure.

Alexander, C., Ishikawa, S., Silverstein, M., Jacobson, M., Fiksdahl-King, I., & Angel, S. (1977). *A pattern language: Towns, buildings, construction*. New York: Oxford University Press.

Alexander, C., & Mehaffy, M. (2015). *A city is not a tree*. Portland, OR: Sustasis Press.

Bergin, J. (2000). *Fourteen pedagogical patterns*. New York: Pace University.

Bruner, J. S. (1960). *The process of education*. Cambridge, MA: Harvard University Press.

DuFour, R. (2010). *Raising the bar and closing the gap: Whatever it takes*. Bloomington, IN: Solution Tree Press.

McTighe, J., & Wiggins, G. (1999). *Understanding by design handbook*. Alexandria, VA: Association for Supervision and Curriculum Development.

McTighe, J., & Wiggins, G. (2005). *Understanding by design* (2nd ed.). Alexandria, VA: Association for Supervision and Curriculum Development.

McTighe, J., & Wiggins, G. (2013). *Essential questions: Opening doors to student understanding*. Alexandria, VA: ACSD.

**FIGURE 4.1** A simple fence separates a viewing area from a wetland

# 4

# BOUNDARIES

By comparison to the big idea or the big questions that we looked at in the previous chapter, boundaries get little attention in contemporary educational discourse. In this short chapter, I offer a gentle correction to that state of affairs, examining boundaries and the ways we demarcate the parts of courses and the parts of units and lessons. I argue that our students need to know what fits in a unit or topic and what does not. And they need to know when units start and end, a question I address in more detail in Chapter 5 on entrances and exits but one intimately connected to how we divide and organize instruction—that is, to boundaries. While arguing that such boundaries serve our students, I will also note that they serve us by preventing our trying to treat the whole world in a unit that, in truth, needs to remain finite.

Most teacher-training programs emphasize the big ideas I discussed in the previous chapter; students need to know the big ideas that drive courses, units, and lessons. As I noted there, this emphasis arises in part because of the popular work of people such as Rick Dufour, Jay McTighe, and Grant Wiggins. But it also arises in part because, intuitively, it makes complete sense. Of course, we want our students to know that this or that idea, process, concept, or chain of events is the whole point of our studying, for instance, chemical compounds, the water cycle, or the formation of the United Nations.

In my introduction to the patterns in Chapter 2, I made reference to Robert Frost's famous poem "The Mending Wall," noting his wisdom that while there is something we may not love about a wall, good fences still make good neighbors. In Chapter 2, I also noted the human propensity to classify and categorize. Our earliest efforts as language-learners to label people and objects are attempts to impose some order on the world in which we find ourselves. The first words out of children's mouths are usually nouns, category names.

We continue that process of categorizing and classifying throughout our lives, in our earliest efforts, erecting linguistic walls between dogs and dolls, in our later efforts perhaps trying to establish whether cougars, panthers, and mountain lions are the same or different species. We do this not only in language. We do it in the physical world. We demarcate nations and regions. We mark out commercial, residential, and industrial zones, as well as utility corridors and school zones. We demarcate one person's private property from the next person's and we divide our homes, schools, and offices into rooms.

With Frost, I want to argue that good fences make good neighbors, even if there is something that doesn't love a wall. This is true in the world of thinking and language and it is true in the physical world and the spaces we inhabit in it. It is likewise true in the world of curriculum, instruction, and assessment, which, metaphorically, are spaces we and our students inhabit in our educational work. Our students need boundaries to help them impose order on their educational world, and our task as teachers may be akin to the language coaching that parents do with their toddlers or the zoning that city councils and planning departments do at city hall.

This chapter focuses on the cognitive and curricular boundaries our students need and how we incorporate those boundaries into course and unit design. Secondarily, it looks at how we can help our students by working within some chronological boundaries. Because this chapter itself must have boundaries, I will omit treating three other kinds of boundaries in it. The professional boundaries we maintain between ourselves and students, while important, do not appear in this chapter (Givens, 2007). Likewise, I do not treat here the boundaries we need to maintain between our work lives and our non-work lives (Palmer, 1998). Third, building a classroom ethos (of one kind or another) requires constant boundary maintenance related to such matters as respect, routines, protocols, and classroom policies (Middleton & Perks, 2014); this one has a robust research conversation of its own, and so I will not treat the question of classroom climate here.

## The Need for Boundaries

The fence shown in Figure 4.1 speaks volumes about the need for boundaries. The area on the other side of the fence requires protection. The residential deck in Figure 4.2 lacks boundaries. Without the railings we ordinarily associate with decks and that local building codes usually require on decks 45 cm above the ground or more, this deck qualifies as a deck only in the barest sense that it is raised off the ground and one can sit on it. It would not qualify aesthetically as a deck anywhere. And it does not qualify as a deck legally in this city and many others. A platform it is, but the socializing and relaxation that the word deck usually connotes, while possible here, would seem somewhat out of character on this unenclosed, undefined surface. The structure itself certainly does not invite

**FIGURE 4.2** A residential deck that lacks boundaries

those activities. Without boundaries, it appears more like the loading dock one might expect to find at the back of a small delivery company. To recall the thesis of Chapter 3 for a moment, lacking the boundaries our minds seek, it also fails to draw our focus to any centre. Its main accomplishment may, in fact, be conceptual and directly related to this book; it demonstrates the importance of boundaries to define spaces.

## Natural and Built Responses to the Need for Boundaries

Everywhere in the world, people erect fences to separate one place from another. The pole fence shown in Figure 4.1 is meant to keep people out of a nature preserve, but no sternly-worded signs warn of prosecution for those who enter the wetland. Animals or people wanting to get through that fence obviously can do so. That simple fence affords no privacy; in fact, the presence of the bench implies that people are supposed to see through and over the fence. Although fragile and permeable, the fence persists because a farmer, a county, or a conservation group erected it and maintains it. It remains necessary because it indicates a boundary.

In the Irish countryside, drystone walls separate fields (Figure 4.11, at the end of the chapter). Built without mortar, they are impervious to weather. Built of carefully stacked stone, they can resist both gravity and the horizontal efforts of animals. They last thousands of years and they accomplish two simple purposes:

they demarcate one field from the next, and they keep animals where they belong. In the construction of these drystone walls, the limits of human will and strength combine so that most walls are short enough to see over. That is, farmers built them only to create boundaries between their fields, not to afford privacy.

Hadrian's Wall (Figure 4.3), which runs east to west across northern England, is an exception to these generalizations about drystone walls, not only because those who built it used mortar. Named after the Roman emperor who commissioned it, it literally was meant to mark the boundary of an empire, something more important to Rome than in which field some British cows grazed. Sections of the wall stand to this day, some of them ranging in height up to six metres. Hadrian's Wall was staffed with garrisons at roughly fixed distances throughout its length, as well as with several major forts. Halfway around the world from England, various emperors built the Great Wall of China, with some sections predating Hadrian's Wall and others appearing later. Both of these walls were meant to indicate imperial boundaries and to protect empires by preventing the entry of foreigners. That neither wall ultimately fulfilled its purpose might be instructive for nations in our own time who believe they can keep the world at bay. Their failures notwithstanding, they do indicate how important boundaries are and how important they seem to human beings.

In cities and towns, we create boundaries for a variety of reasons. Most people do not want to live near the noise and pollution of industry. Many people do not want to live near nightclubs, although some prefer to be within walking distance of them. Cities aim to protect children by reducing automobile speeds near schools and parks, or by prohibiting certain products from being sold within a specified distance of schools. Some of these separations—boundaries—occur naturally because of rivers, hills, ravines, and woods. We build others. Our built

**FIGURE 4.3** Portion of Hadrian's Wall, built about 122AD, demarcating the northern edge of Roman Britain

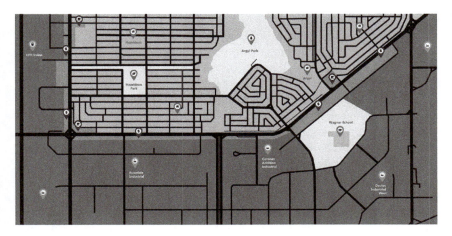

**FIGURE 4.4** A zoning map shows how 63$^{rd}$ Avenue and Argyll Road create a boundary separating industrial land (south, dark gray) from residential and park land (light gray) in Edmonton, Alberta

boundaries include cemeteries, arterial streets and roads, railway tracks, canals, utility corridors, and parks. Arguably, built boundaries include zoning laws. But with the exception of zoning laws, our built boundaries obviously serve purposes other than separating neighborhoods, purposes such as transport and recreation. Our natural boundaries provide space for recreation and they absorb carbon dioxide. Some of them even provide food. Those important functions aside, my interest here is in the simple fact that they divide one part of a town or city from another and that we consider those divisions essential to the quality of our lives.

We also create boundaries within our homes and places of work. Boundaries help transform the spaces in which we find ourselves into places where we feel at home. Designers of houses deal with the same questions faced by designers of towns and cities. We demarcate spaces in buildings for functional reasons: this room has this purpose and that room has that purpose. We demarcate them for structural reasons: partitions in a home can aid in supporting the next floor or the roof. And we demarcate them for aesthetic reasons: a partition would make this structural space feel more comfortable or habitable. Think for a moment about houses built a century or more ago. In such homes, the rooms are clearly demarcated, probably with doorways surrounded by wide, dark moldings. The costs and difficulties of residential heating in poorly-insulated homes dictated this practice, but only to a degree. Cultural patterns were at work too; before televisions or smart phones, being present in a room had a different meaning than it has today. The house where I live now—built in 2004—has the kitchen, dining area, and living area all clustered in a large undivided space. This design has its benefits. It feels open. Light from the windows reaches all parts of the room. Socializing is simplified. Thanks to some bar stools and a high serving-counter, meal preparation can be more of a social affair. But sometimes we would like to eat without seeing the stove and kitchen counter. We would like to talk without hearing the dishwasher. It is clear to me that had the designers of my house read Chapter 4 in this book, they would at least have chuckled about how other generations viewed boundaries before continuing with the open plan concept that the city approved for our house.

Geographers, philosophers, psychologists, theologians, sociologists, and novelists have all made attempts to understand the importance of place to human identity and the role of boundaries in creating those places (examples include Alexander, Anninou, Black, & Rheinfrank, 1987; Auburn & Barnes, 2006; Carson & Pratt, 1956; Dixon & Durrheim, 2000; Stegner, 1986; Tuan, 1974; Wallwork & Dixon, 2004; Wharton, 1897). Regardless of their disciplinary background or philosophical orientation, these explorers of the inner and outer landscape share the goal of understanding why human beings need a place and how we attempt to transform spaces into places.

Whether we think of sibling children or college students wanting to mark out their spaces in a shared room, cubicle workers seeking privacy on a large office floor, or educators wanting a place to work where they cannot be found, we see expressions of the human need for a place of one's own (which I treat in Chapter 8, Public and Private). To find those places—or to make them—we construct boundaries.

Depending on their character, boundaries accomplish several things. I noted above that drystone walls demarcated fields but provided no privacy. Some boundaries are meant to protect, either from animals or from human enemies. Many boundaries are meant simply to mark one space from another. With reference to aesthetics, boundaries help focus attention on the centre, as cropping does for the bison's eye in Figure 4.5 and lines between the individual photographs

**FIGURE 4.5** In photography, cropping creates boundaries. The viewer's focus moves to the bison's eye

**FIGURE 4.6** Internal boundaries bring order to a page of photographs

do in the composition of Figure 4.6. With reference to psychology and sociology, boundaries offer security. In short, we create boundaries for many different purposes, not all of them compatible with each other, but all of them interesting as metaphors for them boundaries we need and create in educational settings.

## Boundaries in Curriculum and Instruction

Within curriculum and instruction, we can distinguish two types of boundaries: conceptual or curricular boundaries and chronological boundaries. Without stretching things unduly, we can work both natural and built boundaries in our physical environment into a metaphor for understanding chronological boundaries in the educational environment. Within a school year, major breaks and holidays obviously create natural divisions—if educators want to recognize and use them— between different blocks of instruction. Within the unit, weekends obviously divide instructional time and we should use these to advantage as well.

Even within the school day, the bell marks out one class period from another. When first used, school bells that separated classes or periods qualified as built boundaries, but they are now so widespread that we can safely consider them natural. They are certainly perceived as such by teachers and students, the main users of school buildings. Like the boundaries themselves, phrases such as "period 2" and "block 4" have become parts of natural language in educational settings and they indicate our acceptance of the boundaries they signify as natural. Still, we should not underestimate the importance of what they mark out for students, even for those not counting down the minutes to the end of the school day. In Chapters 6 and 8, I argue that we should not view these breaks as interruptions. Rather, we should view these breaks as free chronological boundaries and therefore plan the rhythms of our instruction around them. In Chapter 5, I argue that we can introduce new topics and units with high-voltage, grand entrances. Designing instruction so we follow natural breaks with such entrances strikes students as natural. In short, these natural demarcations are a gift to educators, not just because they provide us with some days of rest.

A version of the calendar in Figure 4.7 also appears in Chapter 9 as a possible representation of how students perceive a class where the teacher force-feeds them via direct instruction every day without recognizing or creating any chronological boundaries. In Chapter 9, it functions as an example of stultifying repetition. Here I use it to underline the importance of building internal

| Sun | Mon | Tue | Wed | Thu | Fri | Sat |
|-----|-----|-----|-----|-----|-----|-----|
| 7 | 8 | 9 | 10 | 11 | 12 | 13 |
|  | Take Notes | Take Notes | Take Notes | Take Notes | Take Notes |  |
| 14 | 15 | 16 | 17 | 18 | 19 | 20 |
|  | Take Notes | Take Notes | Take Notes | Take Notes | Take Notes |  |
| 21 | 22 | 23 | 24 | 25 | 26 | 27 |
|  | Take Notes | Take Notes | Take Notes | Take Notes | Take Notes |  |
| 28 | 29 | 30 | 31 | 1 | 2 | 3 |
|  | Take Notes | Take Notes | Take Notes | Take Notes | Take Notes |  |

**FIGURE 4.7** A student's possible perception of four weeks of daily direct instruction without internal boundaries designed into the course or unit

boundaries into courses and units. Without such demarcations, students may perceive a month's instruction in a class simply as one thing after another. Presumably, a history class so structured would fit the variously attributed phrase, *one damn thing after another.*

Turning from chronological to conceptual and curricular boundaries, in educational settings, teachers determine the shape and location of the built boundaries. Built conceptual boundaries can take several forms.

Built curricular and instructional boundaries should help students demarcate and organize their learning; they should not strike students as arbitrarily-timed interruptions. A common question in classrooms where students write tests is, "Will this be on the test?" Although we may not think of that question as a question about boundaries, it is. The student who asks that question is asking about fit and importance (which recalls the discussion in Chapter 3 about centres). Given our teacher idealism, we might wish our students attended our classes only for the joy of learning, but we must admit that after several years in school they have learned that assessment is important. So, to them, this question is completely legitimate. When we recognize it for what it is—a question about boundaries and fit—we may be able to overcome our frustration at hearing it (again!) and instead use it as a teachable moment. A good response to the question might run along the lines of, "What connections do you see between what you are asking about and the driving question or questions of this unit?" or, "Give me two reasons to include this material on the test and two reasons not to include it." The teacher's purpose in giving these responses is not to avoid answering the question. Rather, it is to force the student to reflect on the question of boundaries and fit: does this material belong in the unit or does it not? If it does belong, how and where does it fit? How does it contribute to our attempt to answer the big questions of the unit or our wish to understand the big idea of the unit?

## *Clear and Visible Boundaries for Students*

Some teachers use a wall-sized KWL sheet built by the whole class early in the unit. This acts as a curriculum guide or pacing guide throughout the unit. The teacher and students alike can use this tool to check at any time whether something fits or does not fit within the scope of the unit. The same teacher who dreads the question, "Will this be on the test?" would likely love the question, "May I do a project on lightning as part of this unit on electricity and magnetism?" It is a great question. In that moment, the teacher could respond, "Well, let's look at the KWL sheet on the wall and see if we think it fits or not."

Some teachers rely more on documents. They distribute electronic or paper unit outlines. Some even distribute or make available the actual program of studies published by the jurisdiction. Many students, when they see the curriculum that their teacher must work with, adopt the view that the teacher is more their coach than their judge. Teacher and students together must work so students understand what is required of them. Obviously, this would not work with primary students, but somewhere in the middle years students can begin to be receptive to such documents. To return to the question of doing a project on lightning in the electricity and magnetism unit, the teacher could refer to the program of studies, even challenging the student to show how lightning fits or to discover why it does not.

Like many of my readers, I imagine, I have a strong disaffection for teaching to the test, but many teachers work with their students through old standardized tests, not simply to memorize answers to questions, but to understand the kinds of things that test-makers typically ask about. Some teachers deconstruct the rubrics for major assessments with their students. Again, this is not simply to help students get a higher grade on an assessment but is to help them understand more deeply and wholly what the educators or officials behind that assessment envision as a great formula or a great explanation. What is the connection of these practices to boundaries? Deconstructing a rubric can increase a student's knowledge of what is and what is not a good solution or answer. Examining old exams helps students get a sense of what questions never appear (the three conditions stipulated in the Treaty of Disley) and what ones frequently appear (the chemical effects of coal smoke on limestone buildings). Students want to know what is in and what is out, a boundary question we perhaps wish they could push to the backs of their minds, but one that, in their well-schooled perceptions of the world, remains important.

## Crossing Curricular Boundaries: Interdisciplinarity and Integration

Recall my brief discussion of drystone walls. These were built mostly in rural settings. I noted in my description of that style of building that because the farmers who built those walls had limited energy and time they built them only high enough to serve the two purposes of dividing fields and keeping animals where they belonged. Privacy was not at stake in these walls the way it is with many residential fences today; in fact, farmers needed to have a view of the field in order to see that their animals were present and well. These drystone walls also predated our contemporary understanding of the individual and the private self (Taylor, 1987). Their purpose was simple, and essentially single.

A curricular corollary of these walls that one can so easily talk over interests me. Does my argument that courses, units, and lessons must have boundaries leave us without means for communication between subject areas? I will argue in Chapter 6 that we must make connections between the educational parts and the educational whole and between students' education and their lives. In reference to these drystone walls, I want to argue this metaphor: just as these walls are usually the perfect height for conversation, subject-area boundaries and unit boundaries can be venues for conversation.

Some years ago, in "Resisting Curriculum Integration: Do Good Fences Make Good Neighbors," I wrote that disciplinary boundaries evolved for good reasons and that those who resist interdisciplinarity or integrated education believe they have good reasons for their resistance (2009). For example, astronomers and historians use quite different tests to determine what warrants our attention. Astronomers have ways of testing whether the claim that the moon is made of green cheese is correct. Historians use different approaches to examine the claim that Hitler was bad, not mad. The business of astronomers and historians differs in other significant ways as well, so many in fact that some people conclude that conversation between them is rendered impossible. I argued the opposite view in my "Good Fences" article; I wrote there that we should view disciplinary boundaries not as barriers but as fences built just the right height for interdisciplinary conversation. After all, because we represent different disciplined ways of viewing the world we all want to understand, we actually need each other's perspectives. I will not repeat the article here but can summarize it with two short statements. We need to talk. And we can.

To bring this argument for interdisciplinary conversation to K–12 settings, we might say that while we need boundaries to help make clear what belongs and what does not belong in a given course or unit, those boundaries should be more like the fence near the wetland shown in Figure 4.1 than the walls of Windsor Castle shown in Figure 4.8. When students propose projects or lines of enquiry that lie clearly outside the learning outcomes for our current work, we can use

**FIGURE 4.8** Windsor Castle, Berkshire, England. Boundaries to keep people out

**FIGURE 4.9** The Great Wall of Saskatchewan, Albert Johnson, 1962–1991. Smiley, Saskatchewan

those proposals to clarify the parameters of that work. We can offer that their project would fit if they could agree to keep the current learning outcomes in the foreground and direct significant effort to showing the links between what they propose and the big idea of the unit.

## Boundaries, Entries and Exits

People build boundaries for many reasons. Some are meant to keep people out. Some are meant to mark territory. Some are built in the name of art or whimsy. One farmer's lifelong project ended up with the affectionate name *The Great Wall of Saskatchewan* (Figure 4.9). Albert Johnson started his wall in 1962 simply as a place to get rid of the field-stones he cleared. And he never stopped. His pragmatic objective was to rid his fields of stones, but a philosophical objective emerged over time: he once claimed that everyone should done something significant and useless during their lifetime. Educational work is probably too important to build boundaries in the name of whimsy, but we have other good reasons to build them.

I have argued in this chapter that units need boundaries. Students need to know what fits in and what does not. But they also need to be able to *get in*.

**FIGURE 4.10** The hedge creates a boundary, one that has an entrance

To the degree that instructional units are places, we must design them so that students can find the entrances, and we need to make those entrances inviting so students will want to enter. This takes us to the next chapter's exploration of entrances and exits.

## References

Alexander, C., Anninou, A., Black, G., & Rheinfrank, J. (1987). The personal workplace: A new system of office furniture for the 21st century. *Architectural Record*, 11(September), 130–141.

Auburn, T., & Barnes, R. (2006). Producing place: A neo-Schutzian perspective on the psychology of place. *Journal of Environmental Psychology*, 26(1), 38–50.

Badley, K. (2009). Resistance to curriculum integration: Do good fences make good neighbors? *Issues in Integrative Studies*, 27, 113–127. Retrieved from https://our.oakland.edu/handle/10323/14450.

Carson, R., & Pratt, C. (1956). *The sense of wonder*. New York: Harper & Row.

Dixon, J., & Durrheim, K. (2000). Displacing place-identity: A discursive approach to locating self and other. *The British Journal of Social Psychology*, 39(1), 27–44.

Givens, R. (2007). Mending walls: Recognizing the influence of boundary issues in the teacher/student relationship. *Christian Scholar's Review*, 36(2), 127–141.

Middleton, M., & Perks, K. (2014). *Motivation to learn: Transforming classroom culture to support student achievement*. Thousand Oaks, CA: Corwin.

Palmer, P. (1998). *The courage to teach*. San Francisco, CA: Jossey-Bass.

Stegner, W. (1986). *The sense of place*. Madison, WI: Wisconsin Humanities Committee.

Taylor, C. (1987). *Sources of the self: The making of the modern identity*. Boston, MA: Harvard University Press.

Tuan, Y. (1974). *Topophilia: A study of environmental perception, attitudes, and values*. Englewood Cliffs, NJ: Prentice-Hall.

Wallwork, J., & Dixon, J. A. (2004). Foxes, green fields and Britishness: On the rhetorical construction of place and national identity. *British Journal of Social Psychology*, 31(1), 21–39.

Wharton, E. (1897). *The decoration of houses*. New York: Norton.

**FIGURE 4.11** Drystone walls near Inishmore, Aran Islands, Ireland

**FIGURE 5.1** An inviting entrance at Althabasca Hall, a residence at the University of Alberta, Edmonton

# 5

# ENTRANCES AND EXITS

The teaching challenge I want to explore in this chapter is students' need to know very clearly when units, topics, or themes begin and when they end. The introduction to a course or unit is like the entrance to a building: it must make clear to the passerby where to enter, it must invite that passerby in, and that passerby, once inside, must know how to get out again.

Our own knowledge of our courses and the units in those courses figures as an important element in the context of this challenge. We likely approach a given unit with the whole year in view and with the knowledge that we have gained by having taught that unit several times in previous years. There is a sense in which, to us at least, the unit may be like our native tongue; we do not notice the syntactic or grammatical anomalies in the language we first learned to speak. Our tacit knowledge that this unit typically takes 13 days or 36 days is **our** tacit knowledge, not our students'. We know that we are starting a new unit today, or next Tuesday, and that we need to finish it by the end of October, and on it goes. In short, the teacher typically has not just a clearer idea, but an entirely different understanding of the structure of the year than the student does.

Our students may have no idea what they are getting into. In fact, if we did not end the previous unit in an obvious way, our students may not even know that we have moved on to new material; they might not have even ascertained that the course is divided into units. Our students' varied academic strengths and varying interest in school life itself figure importantly in the context as well. Some of our students attend our classes day to day in a state of relatively ignorant bliss, leaving it entirely to us to decide what they are to work on and when one thing stops and another starts. And of course, other students are keen to get control over their own work; they want dates and times and they want to know what course weight is assigned to various assignments and assessments. Some of these students, even in middle-school, will want to note in their calendar or planner the dates that their work is due. Many of these latter students probably have a clear grasp of the idea that units have beginnings and ends, and if the teacher has announced the date the unit will end, they will have noted that date and planned accordingly.

For all types of students, then, we need clear entrances.

## A Parallel Problem in Design

Cities and towns struggle with the same challenge as educators. In Chapter 4, I noted the role that planning departments play in determining zones. How do they enforce zoning laws when specific individual applications for rezoning seem to rest on compelling arguments? How do they protect residential quiet without causing commute times to grow beyond reason? And, more to the point of this chapter, having separated the city's zones from each other, how do planners make sure that people can get into the areas they need to enter and out of those places when they have completed their business there? I am grateful that I am not in charge of answering these questions (although I believe that educators must answer more difficult questions). Many people more expert than me have debated planning and zoning (for example, Alexander, 1966, 1967; Alexander et al., 1977; Gibberd, 1967) and I will leave it to them to sort these matters out.

**FIGURE 5.2** The entrances to these London townhouses are easy to find

At the level of individual buildings, we need to be able to find the entrances. One can easily spot the entrances to the London townhouses shown in Figure 5.2. The vines distinguish the ground floor from the floor above, and the white window frames differ markedly from the dark doors. In anticipation of my argument in the next chapter, the similar entrances on these homes offer not only a common type of connection to the street, but they also contribute to the overall coherence of the building.

When executed poorly, design can cause confusion. The Biological Sciences building at the University of Alberta has provided generations of students with a source of bleak humor. As shown in Figure 5.3, a major sidewalk leads in from one of the university's main perimeter roads to a blank wall. The main entrance to the building is around the corner to the left of the sidewalk. Arguably, the university could reroute the sidewalk at lower cost than it would take to renovate the building. Among students, urban legends abound about classrooms that can be reached only through closets and staircases that lead nowhere. One hopes that these are only legends. One also hopes that registration in biology courses at this university is easier than entrance to the biology building.

The designers and owners of office buildings, legislature buildings, galleries, museums, religious gathering places, and even automobile dealerships want people to be able to find their entrances. The design of entrances, while important, is not the only factor that invites or repels the passerby. In many buildings, someone at reception welcomes you in—or does their best to look intimidating.

**FIGURE 5.3** A sidewalk leading to a wall at the University of Alberta

In the case of large public buildings, entrances and foyers have even become the subject of scholarly work, with researchers wanting to know how the various combinations of volume and aesthetics affect the psychology of those entering such buildings (Crosbie, 2003; MacLeod, 2005). A full century before Crosbie, MacLeod and others of our contemporaries were exploring how such entrances and spaces work, Edith Wharton was attempting to understand the vestibule, which she viewed as a place of transition from the street to the house (Wharton, 1897, pp. 107–110). In effect then, the entrance does not include just the door or doors. Arguably, it includes the room one first enters upon passing through the door(s) and it includes any people whose work places them somehow in charge of the space that visitors first enter. As a way to understand the beginnings of courses or units, entrances may contain richer fruit than one might think at first.

Inasmuch as schools are buildings, the entrances to schools also may bear on the questions of this chapter. Educational researchers have asked how school entrances affect students' perceptions of school as places to learn (Ogden et al., 2010), which provides a warrant for our metaphorical consideration in this chapter of the entrances to units. One academic journal, in fact, *School Planning & Management*, gives over many pages per year to such questions as accessibility, school safety, signing in, and lockdowns. Others have examined how to negotiate the ground between welcome and safety (Fiel, 2014; Mann Jackson, 2014). The physical aspects of schools—especially their role in welcoming students and making them feel safe—are not central to my project in this chapter, but they clearly relate. I use the word *space* several times in this volume with reference to the curricular and instructional spaces in which teachers and students do the work of teaching and learning. Clearly, we cannot ignore the physical spaces in which they do that work.

Entrances are important in the digital world as well. Web designers use the concept of the *home page* (Figure 5.4). Internet users experience a range of

**FIGURE 5.4** The landing page on a website can repel or invite the visitor

responses to home pages. At the happy end of the continuum, users are completely satisfied when a website's navigation is simple and the information they desire is easy to find. At the other end of the continuum, users can feel completely frustrated when a website seems to hide the simplest, most sought-after information. A truism among designers is that the larger the organization, the worse the website. In anticipation of my treatment of the entrances to instructional units, I ask, will our students experience the home pages of our units with satisfaction or with frustration?

Panayotis Michelis offers a lyrical description of how even the simplest door—perhaps what Jung would call an archetypical door—meets a deep human need:

> . . . the element of the lintel on posts gives the impression of a gate. It separates the world behind it from the world before it, standing between the two not only as a partition (as in the case of a wall) but also as a connection. It invites us to go through it much more eloquently than two isolated pillars could ever do because in passing through this elementary gate we will experience the pleasure of yet another conquest: the fact that the beam has been lifted and laid horizontally over an empty space, the fact that heavy, earth-bound matter is now suspended in the air. This explains the strange joy we feel when we step through a natural opening in a rock, or walk beneath two trees with their upper branches interlocked, or pass under a bridge.
>
> (Michelis, 1977, pp. 221–222)

Michelis continues by discussing how the combination of entry, walls, and roof offers a shelter akin to a heavenly dome over the individual. I noted at the beginning of Chapter 4 that boundaries and entrances complement each other. Like Michelis, I believe the two work in harmony; in the context of the classroom, units must be bounded, but they must also be open.

As we all know from personal experience, the human need for clear entrances is real. Architects and designers have dealt with it for centuries and will continue to do so. We turn now to some of the solutions on offer in the worlds of design and architecture. Following that, we will consider the importance of clear—and even grand—entrances to instructional units.

## Solutions to the Design Problem

Planners, architects, and builders have solved the problems of entrances and exits in a variety of ways, some better than others. Frank Ching's distinction between three entrance designs is a helpful place for educators to begin thinking about the entrance to new topics and units. He distinguishes three categories: "flush, projected, and recessed. Flush entrances maintain the continuity of a wall's surface and can be, if desired, deliberately obscure. Projected entrances

## THE DOOR AS A METAPHOR FOR FAMILY

There are all kinds of doors—from openings without even a flap to make a shield, or openings with strings of cheap beads to give some kind of vague separation from being outside and inside—all the way to heavy, bulletproof, padlocked entrances. When one says the word *door*, many ideas may come to mind.

If the idea of a family being an "open door" is set forth, it is needful to determine what kind of door that is meant to be. Does it have an opening that has no way of being shut, with no need to knock to pass through? Or should there be a deep moat filled with water, a drawbridge which is only down part of the time, with no way of signalling in an emergency? Is a family to be a secret garden with a door hidden under ivy on an old wall, which can only be found if stumbled upon by accident? Is there to be a bell to ring or a knocker with which to knock?

Edith Schaeffer, *What Is a Family?*, p. 211.

announce their function to the approach and provide shelter overhead. Recessed entrances also provide shelter and receive a portion of exterior space into the realm of the building" (1979, p. 257). I assume that deliberately obscure entrances are of no interest to educators. When I first encountered Ching's work, I was not sure the other two types would be either. But he makes an interesting observation about projected and recessed entries. He writes that ". . . the form of the entrance can be similar to, and serve as a preview of, the form of the space being entered. Or it can contrast with the form of the space to reinforce its boundaries and emphasize its character as a place (p. 257).

Many of my readers will have seen posters of doors. Search online for images *of the doors of* and you will see a few hundred such posters (as well as some ancient rock concert advertisements). Why do doors fascinate us so much? Obviously, in one go, they partly solve the problem of the previous chapter—boundaries— at the same time that they are part of the solution to the problem of this chapter—entrances and exits. Doors stop the weather, unwanted animals or insects, and unwanted people. And they also admit. Perhaps this genre of posters reveals something besides the vast variety of kinds and colours of doors: they have an important aesthetic function.

In a building, the entrance is the entrance to shelter, to the place one wants to go. Even simple entrances, such as those in Figure 5.5, bespeak warmth and welcome, despite their being closed. More ornate entrances, such as those in Figure 5.6, while obviously easier to spot within their context, may sacrifice some of the warmth and welcome offered by simpler entrances. Comparing

**FIGURE 5.5** Entrances can be simple and still be clear

**FIGURE 5.6** Grand entrances are easy to find but may strike the passerby as less inviting than simple entrances

physical entrances may yield an important insight for those thinking about designing entrances to units: warmth and welcome may not always be compatible with grand and ornate.

## Solutions in Curriculum and Instruction

Research on students' impressions of classes and teachers should sober anyone believing that the first day of a unit is just another day and not worth the effort required to make a grand entrance. Some research shows that students form lasting impressions of their classes within the first two weeks (Buchert & Laws, 2008). If students do, in fact, make up their minds that quickly, then teachers and professors had best view the first day of a new term or a new unit as an important day. I write this without cynicism; while these findings are, in a sense, about our reputations, they also say something important about the degree of likelihood our students will join us on the learning journey we have planned. We had best design that journey before we plan it.

With this idea of entrances in mind, how would you start, for example, a middle-school social studies unit on France? I recall meeting a middle-school teacher who started her France unit by helping her students imagine that they were actually travelling to France. She arranged the desks with two aisles, like a wide-body jet. She dressed in a blue suit in the style of an Air France flight attendant. She set up a public-address system in the classroom for that day. She handed out the unit outline on a folded, glossy menu card. And, initially at least, she addressed the class in French. I can think of many other ways to launch a France unit, but none of them could possibly match the creativity, energy, and sheer pluck shown by this award-winning teacher.

After this introduction, what percentage of her students would not have grasped that they were starting the France unit? What percentage of her students would not talk about that class when they arrived home that day? And the most telling question: how many students' imaginations and interest does she hook with this launch every year? While serving on the selection committee for an excellence-in-teaching awards program, I read letters from a student and her principal, both of whom mentioned what a highlight that class was for students. She produced what we might call a grand entrance. Without knowing what her students studied in the previous social studies unit, I know that they knew they had started the France unit. Her grand entrance served as a clear and effective transition to this new place that she wanted her students to be. Earlier, I commented that some buildings have a welcoming receptionist and others have an intimidating security guard. For middle-school students, the Air France flight to Paris would serve as the metaphorical equivalent of the receptionist.

Many teachers and schools have found ways to welcome students to new units, not all of them as creative as the Air France flight, but many of them effective. In one secondary school, teachers in several subjects all distribute unit outlines on blue paper (and use blue paper for no other purpose). In that school, "check the blue outline" has become a mantra that even students say to each other. Other teachers use a *connections* sheet on the first day of a unit. Students think of connections between their new topic and the material in previous units, the material in other courses, and events in the world or in their own lives. Connections sheets help students understand that they have entered a new unit, but they also build coherence by connecting the current unit both to previous course work (Chapter 6) and to the students' larger world. Many teachers begin new units with KWL sheets or with one of its many adaptations (Lyman, 1981; Reese, 2015). Some teachers use students' individual KWL sheets to assemble a whole-class KWL chart on the classroom wall. This is meant to guide instruction throughout the weeks of the unit.

Some teachers use multiple starts, giving students some choice in their first assignment in the unit. Some will choose work from their textbook, others will do journal-writing, and others will draw or graph. One way to approach multiple framings of entrances is to use Howard Gardner's concept of multiple intelligences (Gardner, 1983, 1999). In this approach, teachers challenge students to develop projects related to their own strengths and to the new topic, a challenge for which most students need scaffolding. A list of suggested projects for each of the strengths Gardner differentiated will suffice for most students. Some teachers use a diagnostic pre-test on the first day of a unit, informing students that it does not affect their grade but does help both teacher and students know what work remains. Searching *teaching unit starts* online will yield several million results. Many of these records relate to the kinds of entrances we design and build for new units.

I offer two cautions about entrances, the first about incorporating the textbook into the entrance to a new unit. The teacher in a rush might introduce the unit and set the students to work immediately with some textbook reading and the textbook questions that follow that reading. I have written hundreds of textbook questions (for grades 7–12) and have always wished that no teacher would use those questions to introduce a unit. In design terms, a quick introduction followed by textbook work is a simple hole in the wall, not a proper entrance. Students—and teachers—need a more elaborate entrance to a unit.

The second caution is about shortening classes on the first day of term. Many schools give part of the first instructional day over to administrative functions related to registration and to a school assembly. The abbreviated periods that result are too short to allow teachers to execute any kind of grand entrance to a new course. Students' learning energy and whatever excitement they may have had for the new year will be partially dissipated by their not having dug into any of their classes in depth. In short, my entrances argument implies that we should not shorten classes on the first day of school.

## Exits

The title of the chapter included both words: *entrances* and *exits*. I have two main concerns with exits and will deal with them quickly. First (the corollary to my entrances argument), exits should be clearly marked. Students should know that they have completed the unit. The majority of research on *closing* classes points to the educational efficacy of an intentional end to a lesson rather than permitting the bell to end the lesson at whatever point the class happens to be when the bell rings (Bloomquist, 2010). In other words, the lesson has a beginning and an end. While closing the class has become a rich area of research, closing the unit has not. In light of that shortage of research, we can only extrapolate. Intuitively, the parallel makes sense. However, we do not need to rely on intuition alone. A new unit will start, likely on the next class day, and the teacher will want the students to know that the previous unit has ended. We do them and ourselves a favor if we make it clear that the unit has ended.

The teacher can mark the exit in several ways, some of them more administrative, such as retrieving school-owned resources from students or confirming that the teacher's grade record reflects what students actually have done. More substantial examples include poster displays, student-written performance pieces, and culminating presentations.

My second concern about exits is that many educators default to the unit test as the final assessment—on the final day—in every unit. This mechanism clearly marks the unit end, but it may be seem repetitious to students (Chapter 9) and

**FIGURE 5.7** Exits also have the power to invite

unwise pedagogically if it serves only as a summative assessment that produces a grade. Perhaps those teachers wanting to assess by means of a unit test should design the unit so it appears two or three days before the unit closes, leaving time for remediation and further work in those areas students have not yet learned.

## Conclusion

In Chapter 4, I argued that the boundaries of units need to be clearly demarcated so that students know what is in a given unit and what is out. In this chapter I have argued that educators should clearly mark entrances and exits so students know when they have begun and when they have ended their study of a given topic or unit. Furthermore, I argued here that entrances should be inviting, even grand, so the students' imaginations are hooked on the first day. Several times throughout the rest of the book I will mention entrances and exits, for these two matters connect to all the other principles in the book. But, now, we turn our attention in Chapter 6 to coherence and connection.

## References

Alexander, C. (1966). The pattern of streets. *Journal of the American Institute of Planners*, 32(5), 273–278.

Alexander, C. (1967). The city as a mechanism for sustaining human contact. In W. R. Ewald (Ed.), *Environment for man: The next fifty years* (pp. 60–109). Bloomington, IN: Indiana University Press.

Alexander, C., Ishikawa, S., Silverstein, M., Jacobson, M., Fiksdahl-King, I., & Angel, S. (1977). *A pattern language: Towns, buildings, construction*. New York: Oxford University Press.

Bloomquist, T. (2010). *Effectiveness of closure in lesson design: A quasi-experimental investigation*. (EdD dissertation). Newberg, OR: George Fox University.

Buchert, S., & Laws, E. L. (2008). First impressions and professor reputation: Influence on student evaluations of instruction. *Social Psychology of Education*, 11, 397–408.

Ching, F. D. K. (1979). *Architecture, form, space & order*. Reinhold: Van Nostrand.

Crosbie, M. J. (2003). *Designing the world's best: Museums and art galleries*. Melbourne, Australia: Images Publishing.

Fiel, P. V. (2014). Protect the entry to protect the school. *School Construction News*, 17(7), 18.

Gardner, H. (1983). *Frames of mind: The theory of multiple intelligences*. New York: Basic.

Gardner, H. (1999). *Intelligence reframed: Multiple intelligences for the 21st century*. New York: Basic Books.

Gibberd, F. (1967). *Town design* (5th ed.). New York: Praeger.

Lyman, F. T. (1981). The responsive classroom discussion: The inclusion of all students. In A. Anderson (Ed.), *Mainstreaming digest* (pp. 109–113). College Park, MD: University of Maryland Press.

MacLeod, S. (Ed.) (2005). *Reshaping museum space: Architecture, design, exhibitions*. London: Routledge.

Mann Jackson, N. (2014). A safe welcome. *American School & University*, 85(8), 18–19.

Michelis, P. A. (1977). *Aisthetikos: Essays in art, architecture, and aesthetics*. Detroit, MI: Wayne State University Press.

Ogden, H., Upitis, R., Brook, J., Peterson, A., Davis, J., & Troop, M. (2010). Entering school: How entryways and foyers foster social interaction. *Children, Youth and Environments*, 20(2), 150–174.

Reese, J. (2015). *Thinking for understanding: An introduction to the teaching for understanding (TfU) framework Harvard University, Project Zero*. Retrieved from www.qvsd.org/uploaded/District_Files/ProjectZero/Thinking_for_Understanding-QVJan2015.pdf.

Schaeffer, E. (1975). *What is a family?* Old Tappan, NJ: Fleming Revell.

Wharton, E. (1897). *The decoration of houses*. New York: Norton.

**FIGURE 5.8** The clearly-marked entrance to Chinatown in Vancouver, British Colombia

**FIGURE 6.1** The elements on this English street cohere

# 6

# COHERENCE AND CONNECTIONS

The parts of a lesson, unit, or course need to connect to each other in obvious ways. They need to connect to the larger whole of which they are part, the lesson to the unit, the unit to the course, the course to the curriculum. They need to connect outwards to the students' own lives. And all these connections must be obvious to students. Where these connections are clear, coherence results.

This concern for coherence and connection arises out of design and architectural theory, of course. But it has embarrassing, autobiographical roots as well. Like many teachers (and as I admitted earlier in this book), I have had a student state, "I just don't understand how this fits in the course." My under-my-breath, visceral response to such a claim is that the student has failed to grasp what I—obviously a brilliant teacher—have already made perfectly clear. My more reasoned response, usually some moments later, is recognition that my job is to show how the parts fit the whole, not my student's job to figure that out.

As educators, we need to ensure that the parts fit the whole and can easily be seen to do so. That is the challenge of coherence and connection.

## Coherence and Connection in Design

All architects work with the need to locate any given building on its site and connect it to its larger context. In their designs, they may include references to nearby buildings or even historical references, for example to the primary work carried on in a district in a previous era. And they choose windows, doors, and steps to connect the building to its immediate surroundings, so that people outside are drawn in and people inside do not feel isolated from the activities outside.

**FIGURE 6.2** A building that overwhelms its context

Despite what the architecture books say, not all buildings fit their context. Figure 6.2 shows an office building in Vancouver that makes no reference to its immediate context, a small, older hotel. In fact, it sends an almost antagonistic message along the lines of "size matters" or "don't let the door hit you as you leave." Still in Vancouver, Figure 6.3 shows two condominium towers that also fail to make reference to their surroundings. Admittedly, several decades from now, this neighborhood—largely filled with low-rise apartments at the time of the photograph—might have dozens of similar towers and these two buildings will then fit their context. By definition, in neighbourhood transition, one building always has to be first, and that is true in this Vancouver neighborhood. Meanwhile, these two do not fit; they fail to connect to their surroundings and they make no contribution to coherence.

**FIGURE 6.3** Two Vancouver condominiums make reference to each other but not to their context

**FIGURE 6.4** A condominium tower towering over its neighbours

When the city-centre airport in Edmonton, Alberta closed, height restrictions were lifted on a large swath of developed land in and near the city's centre. Figure 6.4 shows one of the results of that rule change, The Regency, a condominium tower 18 or 20 storeys taller than its neighbors. It simply does not fit, although its views of the city and the river below mean that unit prices there are higher than anywhere else in the that area of the city. These Vancouver and Edmonton buildings illustrate the importance of coherence and connection and the truth that contextual fit is an important element in achieving coherence and connection. They also illustrate the truth that some builders choose to ignore this particular rule of good design.

The design field in general deals with the questions of coherence and connections. And examples abound of people getting it right. Notice in Figure 6.5 the continuity between the elements in The Copper Owl's effort to brand itself. The stationery, business cards, note pad, pencils, flash drive, and erasers all work in harmony. Even the ways these six elements are displayed shows coherence. This branding effort is not from the real Copper Owl, which is a pub in Victoria, British Columbia. The fictional Copper Owl portrayed in Figure 6.5 is a tech support company. The coherence in the single image creates enough power that some readers may wish The Copper Owl could become their tech support company.

Shifting from graphic design to residential design, Atsushi Ueda deals with questions of coherence and connection in his account of how designers struggle to make the many parts of the contemporary Japanese house—windows, stairs, storage spaces, verandas, and so on—fit together while honoring Japanese building traditions (1990). Inasmuch as he applies tested and proven principles to the specific challenge of house design, his ideas could easily serve as the foundation for the branding scheme of The Copper Owl. Like most of the works I refer to in this book, Ueda's essay was not intended as a metaphor about course and unit planning. Nevertheless, reading it compels the reflective educator to ask how the parts of our courses fit together.

The state of urban planning is not as bleak as my comment on Figures 6.2, 6.3, and 6.4 might have indicated. Many cities insist that new buildings fit their context, enforcing height restrictions with genuine resolve. After a fire destroyed a century building in a historic shopping and restaurant district called Whyte Avenue, the city of Edmonton insisted that the replacement building fit the context. The two sides of the block in question—one a century old and one a decade old—are easy to tell apart. But the designers' efforts to situate the new buildings (in Figure 6.7) in their context remain evident throughout the design.

Edmonton's success at enforcing height restrictions and historical references along Whyte Avenue goes against the 20th-century trend of ignoring the street and the coherence it can provide. The street suffered from decades of declining importance as a place in its own right. For several decades it became more a place to drive on than a place to live. In the last couple decades, especially in city centres and historic areas, people discovered new possibilities for streets as places. In Chapter 11, I criticize the new urbanist movement because its characteristic streets and houses, which are meant to look a century old, are simply not; they lack the patina and warmth that result from long human habitation. The new urbanists still deserve credit for trying to bring beauty back to the streetscape, an

**FIGURE 6.5** Coherence characterizes a corporate branding effort

**FIGURE 6.6** The century-old context for a new development in Edmonton, Alberta

**FIGURE 6.7** The new development connects to the street

initiative that would please American architect, Philip Johnson. He lamented the disappearance of the street as a place simply to be and he called on us all to ". . . re-create the street as a centering device, instead of the splitting device it has become. . . . Someday people are again going to want processionals, are again going to want to dance in village squares, and when they want them, they will get them . . ." (2002, p. 158). I return to this life-giving vision of the street at the end of Chapter 8 when I ask if the we can strive to make the common parts of our classroom programs more uncommon.

I will end this section with Johnson's vision of the street as a way to build the centre and a way to produce coherence. If we can connect the buildings to the street, we can achieve coherence. The discussion of centres in Chapter 3, as important as it is, does not stand alone. The centre helps build the coherence. The parts need the centre. This claim applies to the design of cities, buildings, and corporate branding efforts. And it applies to the design of curriculum and instruction.

## Designing Instruction for Coherence and Connection

At the beginning of this chapter, I made reference to the need for coherence and connection in curriculum and instruction. Excellent teachers might be able to achieve some of that desired coherence on the fly, while teaching. Teachers with good memories can tie a student's question to something someone else asked about three weeks earlier, making connections. Teachers gifted with what Max van Manen calls *tact* (a highly intuitive knowledge of what to do next in the classroom without needing to reflect), by definition make the right move at most moments of the day, keeping the class going in the right direction and keeping its parts connected (1991). And teachers who can make interdisciplinary connections can often—spontaneously—point out links to other subject areas, to pop culture, or to current events, helping their students build a seamless whole out of the many, sometimes disparate, parts of their school experience. Some teachers possess the first two of these gifts, memory and tact, and many teachers can make interdisciplinary connections. The rest of us need strategies and structures. In what follows, I suggest several.

To begin, the course tour and the course review serve similar functions: they give students the global view. In *A Pattern Language*, Alexander and his colleagues advocate that cities and buildings incorporate high places from which one can see one's surroundings (1977, pattern #62). The idea of high places fits my vision of course design. Where, other than possibly on the opening day, do we design in vantage points from which our students can get a long view? Intuitively, it makes sense that their sense of coherence and connection will increase when they see their academic surroundings. The course centres (Chapter 3) will be visible from these high places. They should be able to spot the boundaries (Chapter 4) and the entrances (Chapter 5) from these viewpoints. The list goes on. Our job becomes to design whole courses and units so that students get opportunities to take in these wider views.

Every K-12 teacher today knows the word *scaffolding* and knows that effectiveness in teaching implies building current learning on the foundation of students' prior learning. The research literature in this idea is vast. It is also old, running back to Dewey (1902, 1938), Ausubel (1967, 1969), and even Piaget (1972). There is no need to explain the idea further to anyone reading this chapter but let me at least flag it as one of the fundamental ways we can help students build a coherent understanding of what they are learning at school.

In the last few years, some educators have begun to use the concept of *throughlines*, themes or dispositional goals that run through a whole course or even a whole curriculum (Reese, 2015). For example, in some schools, environmental care runs through all grades and all areas of instruction. The teacher does not necessarily place environmental care in the foreground in every unit, but it remains in view. With environmental care operating as a throughline, mathematics word problems, for example, whether generated by the teacher or by students, might relate to environmental issues. Obviously, different jurisdictions, schools, and groups of schools will generate differing lists of throughlines, but these lists are meant to produce, among other results, a degree of coherence to the whole K-12 curriculum.

In some respects, throughlines are similar to my own concepts of *threads* and *layers*, although throughlines operate at a more global level and threads and layers consist of specifically allocated amounts of time every day or every few days in class. I define threads as activities that classes attend to for a few minutes two or three times per week (and I return to threads at several points in the book; they run like a thread through this volume). Layers take a few more minutes and are incorporated nearly daily. Threads and layers run like lines through a unit and they help tie classes to each other within the day, they help tie days to a unit, and they help tie units to a course. A thread could consist of a few minutes per day attending to current events or caring for the plants and animals in the room. Some teachers even turn the welcome and attendance routine into an explicit thread, the predictability of which increases students' sense of routine and therefore security. Depending on how much the teacher wanted to give to these two strategies, activities that could qualify as threads or layers could include building skills in meta-cognition, literacy, understanding cartoons, stand-up circle meetings, or even tracking the mathematics of various teams in the playoffs. Classes might give a few minutes every day or every second day to gratitude practices (Howells, 2012), music, art, planning and organization, local geography, technology, silent reading, puzzles, and new vocabulary.

Some teachers ask their students to find links to other units or other courses, another way of making connections and building coherence. This activity becomes a layer as students think of mathematical, scientific, aesthetic, musical, or literary aspects of their current unit (in any given subject area). Building a layer this way contributes to coherence in two or maybe three ways. First, the regular search for links ties the lessons together. Second, this search also ties the course to other courses. Third, it may also send a message to students that their teacher knows they are enrolled in other courses and thinking about other subjects. In that possible message is implied another message: my teachers care about the rest of my life and that my education fits into my life. I noted above that some teachers have a kind of interdisciplinary ability or bent. A good argument could be made that teachers should not do that work if when students do it the process enriches their education.

Some teachers go well past allowing their students to look for or make such links between their courses and other courses (what some call horizontal integration). Some specify optional interdisciplinary assignments in their unit outlines so that students themselves can take the lead on finding connections. In my own social studies courses, I called these "math connections," "science connections," and so on. A student wanting to follow up a math connection in a social studies unit, for example, might gather statistics related to the unit's contents and then make poster-sized graphs with the statistics, projected trends, and even speculations writ large for the class to see. Encouraging students to make them brings the connections before the class and increases the degree to which students can shape a place of their own (Chapter 8: Public and Private).

Many elementary teachers use scheduled body breaks as a thread, always getting their students up and moving about 11:00, just before the last class preceding lunch. A secondary teacher I know exclaims daily, "Do you know what I learned on the internet last night?" Her students have come to look forward to her latest revelation from the web, in part because these revelations are interesting, but in part because the thread of what she learned gives consistency to their weeks and months. In my discussion of healthy repetition in Chapter 9,

I note that consistent routines connect one class to the next and one day's instruction to the next. By doing so, they deepen students' sense of coherence, that their education is all of one piece.

Viewed as a layer, meta-cognition warrants closer inspection. Most teachers think about meta-cognition and try to address it. Some secondary teachers talk about it with their students, calling it by name; teachers of younger students simply call it thinking about thinking. One secondary teacher showed me the meta-cognition outline she distributes to her classes on the second day of each semester. She defines the term and tells students why she wants to be explicit about incorporating meta-cognition into her courses. She divides it into five strands and describes it to students this way:

- increasing your awareness of your own personality and learning tendencies, intentionally strengthening your weaknesses and learning how to draw on your strengths;
- intentionally developing your awareness and ownership of course structure and planning, corporately developing classroom expectations, and under-standing responsibilities and freedoms;
- intentionally increasing your understanding of how assessment works and learning how to use it to enhance learning;
- critically assessing your own level of literacy, intentionally strengthening your weak areas and learning new strategies;
- intentionally strengthening your skills in research and writing to prepare you for a lifetime of successful research.

Under each of the strands, she lists several areas and activities that the class will focus on during the term. The topics she includes in strand 1, which she labels *Learning Styles, Personality and Intelligence,* include these: learning styles, personality types, brain research, multiple intelligences, and social cognition. She has students fill out online questionnaires and then uses Think–Pair–Share to engage them in discussion about optimal learning strategies. Under strand 4 (literacy strategies), she lists test-taking strategies, three-column Plus–Minus–Interesting sheets, concept-maps, Venn diagrams, and SOS (Summary–Opinion–Support) sheets. She always reminds her students that she knows they might have used some of these strategies before. But she explains that she wants to situate the teaching-learning strategies she uses in this particular frame, so they will know that while she is concerned about the materials specified in the curriculum, she is also concerned that they strengthen their ability to think about how they think.

Many teachers distribute course and unit outlines as a way to help students see the connections between parts and whole. In the last few decades, the course outline has moved to lower and lower grades, and for good reason; as a means of getting control over and making sense of their education, students want to know what they are going to learn. In concert with this migration, the unit outline has moved downward as well. At the turn of the millennium, middle-school teachers saw some students copy important dates down in their planners. In the years during which those planners became smartphones, the age of the students making such notes to themselves has dropped. Those in the tradition of Neil Postman who lament the disappearance of childhood (1982) have their own concerns about why lower elementary students need to use planners (concerns I share), but my point here is that students want to know what they are going to be learning and when their work will come due. Having important dates in hand (literally if they never let go of their phones) offers a kind of coherence to the students who want to do longer-term planning. Educators who stick to the dates they publish earn the respect of their students. Students who do not know or cannot predict what is coming next experience fear and disempowerment, eventually becoming cynical. Student self-efficacy connects in part to their believing that school makes sense. Course and unit outlines with dates that do not arbitrarily bounce around increase students' belief that school makes sense, and their sense that, at bottom, their education has a kind of coherence. We need to contribute to that.

The provision of course and unit documents to younger students leads to an interesting and sobering observation about higher education. The syllabus in higher education has grown significantly over the last few decades, now typically including required paragraphs about plagiarism, accommodations, attendance, the university's definitions of each grade, and so on. Many professors now include rubrics for each assignment. Both students and professors have witnessed the growth of the syllabus, and both must take some responsibility for its growth. I find interesting that at the same time professors have taken so many steps to provide more detail about course requirements and policies, the idea of unit planning has not been taken up more widely in higher education. Students in higher education could gain similar kinds of comfort and control over their learning—and a greater sense of coherence—if their professors followed the lead of K-12 educators. To their credit, many professors do. But many do not, instead, viewing the whole term or semester as a succession of days during which they will work through their material. The winds of change are blowing in higher education, but they are mostly the cold winds of tighter budgets and more precise assessment instead of the warm winds of learning power and efficacy.

## Conclusion

The parts of the lesson need to cohere with the rest of the lesson. If the lesson is a building on the street called the unit, then it needs to connect with that unit in clear ways. If the unit is a building on the street called the course, then it must connect to that street. Teachers need to remind their students regularly of the

# CONNECTING TO THE STREET OF STUDENTS' LIVES

Current events and popular culture are two ways to connect classroom life to students' lives outside of school. Plenty of online resources describe creative ways to incorporate current events into subject areas. I have already noted that a few minutes' attention to current events could constitute a thread or layer.

One finds fewer suggestions about the pedagogical uses of the occasional reference to popular culture. What I suggest may be a sleight of hand, but teachers who periodically refer to pop culture during direct instruction or discussion with students will keep their attention longer. Almost any direct reference to their music, television, movies, and social media will send several messages to students, among them "This teacher is relevant." Recognizably, the relevance of the course contents—not the teacher—remains our concern, but students seem willing to let teachers get away with this stealth. Somehow population histograms become more palatable if the teacher periodically drops the name of the latest pop icon enjoying his or her fifteen minutes. The sideways allusion and the understated reference have smaller effects on the whole class because many will not make the connection. But these quieter echoes from life outside school have a more intense effect on the few with whom they register; they conclude that the teacher is hip, and they think they are smart. Having students think they are smart rarely hurts instruction.

Sometimes, when allusions to pop culture work, students sense a sudden need to talk to their neighbour, interrupting instruction. To employ such references most effectively, teachers need to learn to keep going, and they may need to train their students to hear such allusions without having to chat with someone nearby simply because the allusion brought something to mind. The inverse of this is also true. When an allusion fails to fire—when no one gets it—teachers need to avoid the temptation of asking why; they need to keep right on teaching.

Not all teachers are equipped or disposed to make references to popular culture. But all teachers have the duty of finding out for themselves how their teaching areas connect with life. All the parts of every course do not connect in obvious ways to students' day-to-day lives but if we cannot see for ourselves or explain somewhat satisfactorily to our students how a course has value in their larger scheme of things, then I sincerely think that we are in trouble and perhaps ought not to include that course in the program of studies, or perhaps ought not to be teaching ourselves.

ways that each unit connects to the other units on the street and to the whole street. Finally, we need to connect and help our students connect what we ask them to do in our classrooms to the larger streets of their lives outside school. When we make or help them make these kinds of connections, they see more clearly the importance of school and the coherence that their education has with the larger world in which they live. One school I know of asks that every assignment be real work for a real audience in the real world. What an inspiring slogan to remind educators that we need to lead our students into important work! Imagine students holding street demonstrations where they insisted that we increase the value of our assessments, not be assigning more grades but by enhancing the connections to and coherence with their lives.

In his book, *Town Design* (1967), Frederick Gibberd borrows a concept from drama and television, the open fourth wall, to describe the public space that draws the landscape into the city. I will borrow from the borrower here and argue that our curriculum, our instruction, and our assessment need an open fourth wall so that students connect the work they do in our classrooms to the lives that they live and to the larger world. Of course, the classroom program focused entirely on being relevant to students' lives and the larger world may lose its centre. But my sense is that most teachers are not going to let things go that far. Let us open the fourth wall enough so that our students become convinced there are good reasons to learn all they can while they are with us.

**FIGURE 6.8** A student demonstration in kentopia

# References

Alexander, C., Ishikawa, S., Silverstein, M., Jacobson, M., Fiksdahl-King, I., & Angel, S. (1977). A pattern language: Towns, buildings, construction. New York: Oxford University Press.

Ausubel, D. P. (1967). *Learning theory and classroom practice*. Toronto, ON: Ontario Institute for Studies in Education.

Ausubel, D. P. (1969). *Readings in school learning*. New York: Holt, Rinehart.

Dewey, J. (1902). *The child and the curriculum*. Chicago, IL: University of Chicago.

Dewey, J. (1938). *Experience and education*. New York: Macmillan.

Gibberd, F. (1967). *Town design* (5th ed.). New York: Praeger.

Howells, K. (2012). *Gratitude in education: A radical view*. Boston, MA: Sense.

Johnson, P., Payne, R., Lewis, H., & Fox, S. (2002). *The architecture of Philip Johnson*. New York: Bulfinch Press.

Piaget, J. (1972). The epistemology of interdisciplinary relationships. In L. Apostel, G. Berger, A. Briggs, & G. Michaud (Eds.), In *Interdisciplinarity* (pp. 127–139). Washington: Organization for Economic Cooperation and Development Press.

Postman, N. (1982). *The disappearance of childhood*. New York: Delacorte Press.

Reese, J. (2015). *Thinking for understanding: An introduction to the teaching for understanding (TfU) framework*, Harvard University, Project Zero. Retrieved from www.qvsd.org/uploaded/District_Files/ProjectZero/Thinking_for_Understanding-QVJan2015.pdf.

Ueda, A. (1990). *The inner harmony of the Japanese house*. New York: Kodansha International.

van Manen, M. (1991). *The tact of teaching: The meaning of pedagogical thoughtfulness*. Albany, NY: SUNY Press.

**FIGURE 6.9** A building connected to its context

**FIGURE 7.1** Central Park in New York City

# 7

# GREEN SPACES

Cities and towns build parks because people need spaces to rest and breathe. Some of these parks take advantage of natural features such as hills and streams. Others are purpose-built, some of them simply fitting into the grid-pattern of the surrounding city. Some, like Central Park in New York City (Figure 7.1), become iconic, as significant as the tallest skyscrapers as symbols of their respective cities. Regardless of origin, shape, size, or even fame, they share the purposes of recreation and restoration for those living nearby. National parks and forests, wetlands and conservation areas, historical sites, and cultural sites serve purposes that overlap with those of the parks found in towns and cities. In some cases, they serve as green spaces on a grander scale than is possible in town. In other cases, while not green, they still allow people to step back from the routines of daily life. In this chapter, I argue that teachers and students alike need spaces to breathe, especially during units with masses of material in which instruction stretches over several weeks.

## A Teaching Challenge in its Context

Consider the academic calendars shown on the next three pages. As educators, we have our own ways of thinking about school calendars. For the first calendar, most of us will agree that the two long weekends in February will be a good break, especially the one in late February when we will have already been back to school for six weeks. Pedagogically speaking, the Martin Luther King Day holiday is a bit early; we will barely have got back into the rhythms of school after the break. It would be hard to launch the new calendar year and then face the slight decline in student learning energy that accompanies the long weekend. We might not completely lose the Friday and Tuesday, but neither we nor our students will be as fully engaged in the work of teaching and learning as we might be otherwise. These are the kinds of things that come to mind when we glance at this calendar.

Now, imagine being a student in one of the schools with those timetables. To recall a comment in Chapter 3, imagine the user's experience.

In the seven weeks following the return to school on January 8, our American students get a long weekend. They get a second long weekend if they live in one of the states that celebrate Presidents' Day on the third Monday in February. Between those two they get yet another long weekend because of a school- or

| Sun | Mon | Tue | Wed | Thu | Fri | Sat |
|---|---|---|---|---|---|---|
| 7 | 8 | 9 | 10 | 11 | 12 | 13 |
| 14 | 15 ML King Day | 16 | 17 | 18 | 19 | 20 |
| 21 | 22 | 23 | 24 | 25 | 26 | 27 |
| 28 | 29 | 30 | 31 | 1 February | 2 Teacher's Prof Day | 3 |
| 4 | 5 | 6 | 7 | 8 | 9 | 10 |
| 11 | 12 | 13 | 14 | 15 | 16 | 17 |
| 18 | 19 President's Day | 20 | 21 | 22 | 23 | 24 |

**FIGURE 7.2** An American student's calendar for the first weeks of the new calendar year

district-wide professional development day for teachers. Our youngest students do not have some kind of mental calendar or picture like the ones on these two pages; for the most part, they go along with the world they live in without overthinking their schedules, and they mostly do what they are told. But, from January 8 onwards, a 10-year old or a 16-year old will certainly be thinking ahead to these long weekends.

Our Canadian student might well see the calendar in Figure 7.3 (in fact, many students where I live did see this calendar in January, 2018). We Canadians love our long weekends, and some decades ago most Canadian jurisdictions created a

| Sun | Mon | Tue | Wed | Thu | Fri | Sat |
|---|---|---|---|---|---|---|
| 7 | 8 | 9 | 10 | 11 | 12 | 13 |
| 14 | 15 | 16 | 17 | 18 | 19 | 20 |
| 21 | 22 | 23 | 24 | 25 | 26 | 27 |
| 28 | 29 | 30 | 31 | 1 February | 2 | 3 |
| 4 | 5 | 6 | 7 | 8 | 9 | 10 |
| 11 | 12 | 13 | 14 | 15 Teacher's Convention | 16 Teacher's Convention | 17 |
| 18 | 19 Family Day | 20 | 21 | 22 | 23 | 24 |

**FIGURE 7.3** A Canadian student's calendar, January/February, 2018

February holiday simply to break the long stretch of work from New Year's Day until Easter, or in the case of some school jurisdictions, from the return to school until spring break (which varies across Canada). Again, how does our student perceive the calendar? Simply put, our student likely sees 28 straight days of school, followed by a wonderful five-day weekend. Barring the presence of green spaces during those 28 days, they are quite likely to ask, "Can't we slow down?"

Those 28 straight days lie behind my assertion that school years, terms, semesters, and even single units need breaks for the same reason that cities need parks. And students need breaks just as much as teachers do. This need intensifies in programs of study that prescribe only three or four units in an academic year, yielding unit lengths of 40 or 50 days. Those units may involve our students learning a succession of difficult concepts. As Figure 7.3 shows, the calendar itself implies some long stretches of school days. And, by definition, we will end up teaching units toward the end of the academic year, when both teachers and students may find their energy flagging. I have noted several times in this volume that the move toward teaching to *the big idea* or *the big questions* was a needed one. However, it is also possible that when teachers focus on the big idea and how much we need to get done (or how important an assessment is), we may tend to work, work, work, and not to rest. This might not be the most encouraging metaphor, but teachers can come to think that they must keep pushing a freight train and doing so means there can never be a moment's rest. That said, students get tired of simply working and working, and when they are called on to do so, they may remain present in the physical sense but become decreasingly so in the cognitive sense.

Most students know teachers who steadily push their students and who regret "losing" a day's instruction. And they know that most of these teachers come to class each day confident about their students' ability to complete all the sections specified in the curriculum documents. By any measure, these are good teachers and, I suspect, they are the kinds of teachers who read a book like this. I write this section on green spaces so such teachers can get a deeper sense of permission to back off periodically so that our students will stay present in both senses.

Teachers and students working this hard need opportunities to breathe. In the midst of all this work, green spaces are a way to humanize the scale of what we are doing (Chapter 10) by breaking the large unit into smaller parts, the same way we break a course into units, themes, or topics.

## Breathing Room: A Parallel Problem in Design

Teachers need their students to learn what their respective jurisdictions require. Many individual educators work day-to-day with a sense that the academic year is not long enough, in the same way that curriculum committees in schools of education often wish they could add one or more years to the typical teaching degree. Town and city planners face a parallel problem; they face a similar pressure to make everything fit. And some of the necessary functions or aspects of cities do not fit well near others (industrial near residential, for example). Land and infrastructure costs compel planners to fit as many buildings into every square kilometer of space as is reasonable. Whether a particular area is zoned as residential, commercial, or industrial, the density challenge remains the same. The meaning of the word *reasonable* is important here. Planners need to take into account transport or parking, other services, and the mental health of those who will occupy a space. Employing several thousand people in one office tower makes for efficient land use, but efficiency of land use is not the only consideration. Planners need to ask about other services. For instance, if a significant percentage of those people want to get out of their building at lunch, what can they do? Is there food nearby? Is there a gym? Are there spaces to sit? Are there walking trails nearby? People working in tall buildings need to find ways to release the tension of work.

The Sibuya intersection in Tokyo (Figure 7.4) remains one of the world's busiest. During peak times, up to 1000 people may cross this intersection in one cycle. It thus serves as a symbol of the need for green spaces in the same way that Central Park serves as a symbol of the provision of green spaces. Taken as

**FIGURE 7.4** Sibuya intersection in Tokyo

The feature film *Waydowntown* captures the human need for green space by following the lives of four young office workers who bet each other a month's salary that they can survive a month without stepping outside of their respective office towers (Burns, 2005). With housing, shopping, gyms, and work-places all connected, there is, in principle, no need to step outside. As it happens, filming took place in Calgary, a city with a *Plus 15 Network* of walkways and bridges that actually connects dozens of buildings 15 feet above the ground (you can find a map of it online). As the film proceeds and the fictional month grinds on, the workers involved must deal with their increasing desire to step outside momentarily, or even to run screaming from their offices. This film offers a powerful portrayal of the human need to get outside.

two corollary symbols, these two places catch one of the tensions for educators who think about green spaces. Intensely developed areas like the Sibuya district contribute significant amounts of tax revenue for the city. Central Park does not (although the buildings near it do). City planners must be able to see the non-financial, but very important, longer-term benefits of green space. Later in the chapter, I will argue that teachers also need to be able to see the longer-term benefits of green space, that, designed correctly, green spaces are anything but lost instructional time.

## Solutions to the Design Problem

Planners and architects have found several answers to the challenge of including needed places to breathe in their designs for towns, cities, and buildings. In a city, a green space could mean a pocket park that takes up only a small triangle of space near a corner, with only two benches and a fountain or a small area of lawn. It could mean a whole city block given over to a children's playground, an open area, and a baseball diamond. It could mean kilometers of river valley with bike paths and walking or ski trails. It could mean a promenade along the sea wall with stainless-steel handrails or a completely undeveloped ravine. Even a small space between buildings, such as that shown in Figure 7.5, qualifies as a green space.

I recall when friends were showing me around Oxford their asserting, "You must see the backs!" I did not know what they meant, but I soon found myself in the seclusion of the backs of the respective colleges, strolling on grass next to the river. Christopher Alexander, whose work I mention throughout this book, viewed the quiet backs of these colleges as the paradigm example of green spaces (1977, sections 59, 60, 64, 71, 106). He and his colleagues, in fact, call for areas away from the street, either in the backyard or in a courtyard, where the residents of a home are able to get away from the noise and bustle of the street.

Near or inside a building, green spaces—while likely not literally green—could range from the coffee or lunch room to the kind of grand foyer or entry hall I discussed in Chapter 5. Some work-places may offer a balcony, terrace or roof garden. In others, employees may have access to a simple picnic-table on a small patch of lawn at the back of the property. Employees in an organization may still talk about work in those spaces, but they also talk about family and friends, weekend plans, current events, and sports. In fact, one unwritten rule of many work-places is that no one should talk about work too much during break. A second such rule that governs work-places is often that managers cannot take their break in the same place as the workers. One criterion for the concept of *green space* emerges from that brief list: activities people engage in there are very likely different from work.

Some workplaces lack a literal green space, but breaks have the same function and, in many cases, the same social rules about conversation topics. Construction workers may leave the construction site to drink their coffee in their truck. Or they may sit down somewhere in the project itself for their break, their lunch-pail sitting in front of them on the unfinished concrete floor. Workers in several other industries follow similar routines because transport from the work-site would take too much time. The need for rest breaks—typically two coffee breaks

**FIGURE 7.5** Small green spaces between buildings offer calm and quiet

and one lunch break in a full shift—is reflected in labor laws in most jurisdictions (on this point, it is worth noting that many educators, if they supervise recess, get no formal break in the morning and often work with students or prepare instruction through lunch).

## Finding Breathing Room in Classrooms

As educators, we do not need to wear ourselves and our students out with unceasing work. Even in the most substantive courses, we can build in green spaces and places in which to pull back a bit. In *A Pattern Language*, Alexander and his colleagues suggest that no one in a city should live farther than 300 meters from a green space. Different people may think of different educational applications for that assertion, but I suggest here that every student should be within three or four instructional days of a break.

In what follows I suggest six curricular and instructional approaches and one classroom-layout approach to this need to breathe, starting with the major break. Following that, I will treat the minor break that an educator could take within a single class period. Then I look again at what I called threads and layers in Chapter 6, those few minutes every day or two that are given consistently to a topic or classroom need. My fourth suggestion will be for the teacher to identify in advance the most fun or inherently interesting lesson formats in their teaching repertoire and to use them at those points where, from experience, they know students typically need a break. Fifth, I point to variety and contrast (Chapter 9) as forms of green space. Second last, I suggest designated work periods. Finally, I suggest a literal quiet area in the classroom.

### The Major Break

Several times a year, many teachers find that the backlog of classroom materials and—what is the technical term? . . . *stuff*—builds up to such a mass that the simplest solution seems to be to employ about a dozen students all at once to help get it to where it belongs. Some teachers identify a major break day, giving students the option of doing homework from any class or of helping them with their administrative and classroom tasks. Some students put materials back where they belong. Others takes the recycling out. Another carries a cardboard file box to the teacher's car. Others carry texts to the storage room while another delivers laminating to the school office. In-service teachers will be very familiar with this sort of day. Framed as a green space, this administrative/errands day need not be a source of teacher guilt. It can serve as a green space between units or mid-unit. It is a welcome change of pace (Chapter 9: Repetition and Variety), especially for a class that has been pushing hard. It allows students to work in a bit noisier mode for one day. Typically, during one of these sessions, a few students will ask to work outside the classroom door or in the library. A few will just chat and work half-heartedly, a justifiable mode if the day is truly a break day for a class that ordinarily works hard. A few students will jump at the chance to get outside (recycling, the trip to the teacher's car). The most brilliantly organized teachers in the world never need these days. Mere mortals like the rest of us struggle to keep on top of classroom housekeeping. Teachers' days are full, and to the degree that a teacher's year consists of a long succession of teachers' days, the housekeeping backlog should surprise no one. Meanwhile, students love helping with the housekeeping tasks.

In Chapter 13, I argue that teachers should build *margin days* into every unit. When instruction does not proceed on the anticipated schedule, margin days allow the teacher to make up for delays within the weeks allotted for the unit instead of falling farther and farther behind as the year progresses. If instruction proceeds as anticipated, then the margin day is available for extra tutoring with those who need it and for the kinds of activities I described in the paragraph above. Margin days are not accidental or left-over time that results from bad planning; they are designed into the unit intentionally. When instruction goes to plan, and a margin day does open up, not only does it allow teachers and students to catch up on some work, but it also contributes to positive classroom climate because of the message it sends students about our attitude toward them and our understanding of their work and stress (which I deal with further in Chapter 12).

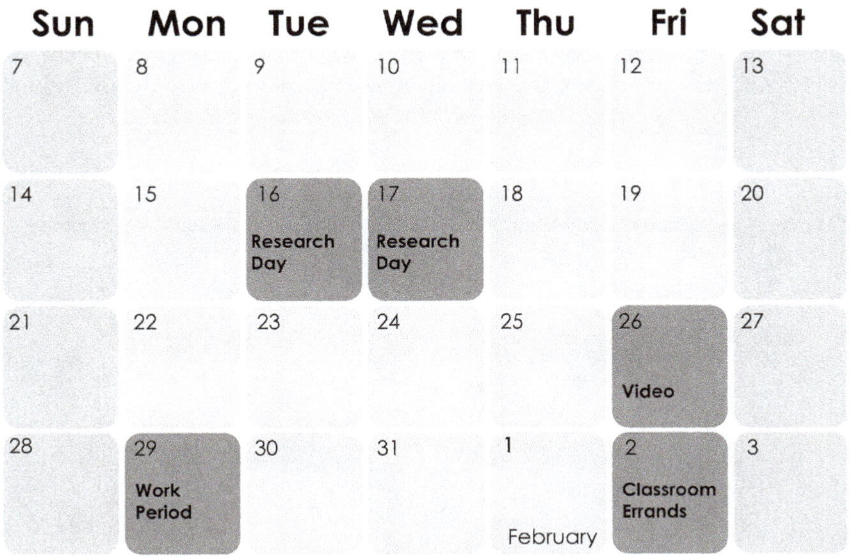

| Sun | Mon | Tue | Wed | Thu | Fri | Sat |
|-----|-----|-----|-----|-----|-----|-----|
| 7 | 8 | 9 | 10 | 11 | 12 | 13 |
| 14 | 15 | 16 Research Day | 17 Research Day | 18 | 19 | 20 |
| 21 | 22 | 23 | 24 | 25 | 26 Video | 27 |
| 28 | 29 Work Period | 30 | 31 | 1 February | 2 Classroom Errands | 3 |

FIGURE 7.6 A portion of the Canadian student's calendar shown in Figure 7.3 with three kinds of green spaces meant to release pressure in the middle of a long stretch of class days

## *The Minor Break*

Everything suited to the major break can also happen within 15 or 20 minutes, and the teacher recognizing that her class needs a small break has many more means at her disposal. She can announce a few minutes of desk-work time, a circle meeting, a body break, or some stretching exercises. Again, I have more interest here in how we frame this than I do in listing all the possible options. Our framing of it has a great deal to do with student learning energy, which varies throughout the year, throughout the week, and even throughout a single class period. Based on the work of Patrick Parrish, I argue in Chapter 13 that we need to take seriously our students' energy trajectory (2008, 2009). When we recognize the human need for green spaces and the simple reality that learning energy fluctuates, we can accept without guilt that a minor break is simply an instructional necessity.

## *Threads and Layers*

Throughout this volume I advocate that we build threads and layers into our unit designs. By thread, I mean a minor activity, focus, or theme to which the class gives two or three minutes most days. By layer, I mean an activity, focus, or theme to which the class gives five or ten minutes each day. Threads and layers contribute to coherence and connection (Chapter 6). They can provide a form of healthy repetition (Chapter 9: Repetition and Variety). They allow students to engage in some smaller-scale content in a class that may be addressing large-scale concepts or topics (Chapter 10: Gradients, Harmony, and Levels of Scale). And, to my point in this chapter, they offer another way to build green

| Sunday | Monday | Tuesday | Wednesday | Thursday | Friday | Saturday |
|---|---|---|---|---|---|---|
| 7 | 8 | 9 | 10 | 11 | 12 | 13 |
| 14 | 15 | 16 | 17 | 18 | 19 | 20 |
| 21 | 22 | 23 | 24 | 25 | 26 | 27 |

**FIGURE 7.7** A portion of a unit design showing the structure of a layer. The teacher did not use the layer on the 11th, 17th, or 25th

spaces into long stretches of instructional days. In Chapter 6, I list typical examples of topics and activities suited to threads and layers.

With reference to providing green spaces, some activities suited to layers and threads, such as building vocabulary, do not immediately strike most teachers as candidates for green spaces, especially compared to carpet time, video clips, couch time, body breaks, board game cafés, cartoon books, or daily care for the plants and animals in the room. However, searching for *classroom vocabulary building fun* just now yielded nearly half a million web pages; clearly, other educators have found ways to give time to vocabulary that students will view as green space. Sustained silent reading is another example of an activity that feels like a break to most students but whose educational value has been established. Professional rewards are available for all teachers willing to design educational and engaging threads and layers into their instruction.

The most widely-used layer in the world is work time, and for good reason. Different teachers and different jurisdictions approach homework and its corollary—in-class work time—in different ways and I will not enter into that debate here. But from the restricted perspective of the need for green space, work time in class makes complete sense. Because of students' different average attention spans (at different ages), blocks of classroom time need to be broken up into smaller parts. A teacher can design a unit so that students enjoy work time (green space) every day (Chapter 9: Repetition), but at different times in class on different days (Chapter 9: Variety).

Humor may work as a thread, but only if the teacher is genuinely capable of humor. For those teachers who truly have wit, humor breaks up stretches of instruction. A doctoral dissertation awaits the researcher willing to compare declining or sustained engagement levels over time for elementary, secondary students, and adults who are listening to direct instruction. The independent variable in this project would be the instructor's ability level for genuine humour. In Chapter 12, I offer a caution about humour, specifically with reference to the Mr. Keating role played by Robin Williams in *Dead Poets Society*.

## Engaging Teaching/Learning Strategies

Several times in this volume, I note with thanks that educators have begun to focus more on learning outcomes. In Chapter 3, for example, I argued that *backwards by design* and my own model meet at the question of centers, or the big idea or big questions. Having praised McTighe and Wiggins and others who have asked us to focus our attention in that (right) direction, I remain concerned that in focusing on content or ideas that way we will ignore the importance of great teaching-learning strategies. All teachers have a repertoire of strategies, some of them highly engaging; I argue that we should design instruction so that we bring out those highly engaging strategies on the days when they are most needed. In my argument for clear—even grand—entrances in Chapter 5,

I suggested that high-voltage strategies are perfectly suited for the first day of a new unit. In Chapter 13, I will argue that we should use higher-energy strategies on days when we know student energy will be lower.

Here, I propose that we use our most interesting learning strategies on the days when we believe or know that we and our students will need a break. Perhaps this day is half-way through a unit or at the mid-point of an unbroken stretch of scheduled school days. To design several weeks of instruction the way I am describing, with higher-voltage lessons strategically scheduled, rather than simply planning what to do day after day, we may need to ignore the sensible, logical order in which the textbook presents the material. Another approach is to stick with the logical order of the material and adapt a high-energy strategy to the content. The goal should be that the students will enjoy the class so much that most will not view it as a work day.

My own repertoire of strategies includes a lesson format which I have used in literally dozens of different situations. I call it *poker chips*. Working with one or two partners, students must agree on how important various factors are or were in, for instance, shaping education, causing poverty, or leading to World War 2. I distribute written instructions and 30–40 poker chips to each pair or trio of students in the room and ask them to indicate their thinking by assigning as few or as many chips as they wish to each category. When they complete their discussion and have assigned all their educational tokens (as we jokingly call them) they enter their totals for each category onto a spreadsheet that shows on the classroom screen. That way we can quickly move into discussion about why so many groups allocated no chips to this category, or just one to this category, or so many to that category. This lesson has never not worked. Some of the most intense discussions I have seen in classrooms happen at the tables, in part because Maria Montessori was right when she wrote a century ago that students think differently when they use manipulatives, and in part because students have only a finite number of chips with which to negotiate and compromise on the way to agreeing with their discussion partners about their views. The sheet of paper shown in Figure 7.8 calls on students to think about an important question: "What drives Alberta classrooms?" Education professors could devise a dozen ways to ask pre-service teachers that question. Asking them to represent their conversation with table partners with a small number of poker chips generates deep discussion; it is a high-energy activity. In this case, the activity has a second stage. After we have seen and discussed the class's thinking about what does drive classrooms, we do a second round, asking this question: "What *should* drive classrooms?" The contrasting numbers between "what *does*" and "what *should*" always make for engaging discussion. That class feels to students like a green space, despite our having taken on heady content that touches on the *School Act*, philosophies of education, teachers' own ideals for their classrooms, and other equally important issues.

**What Actually Drives Most Teachers' Classroom Programs in Alberta Schools?**

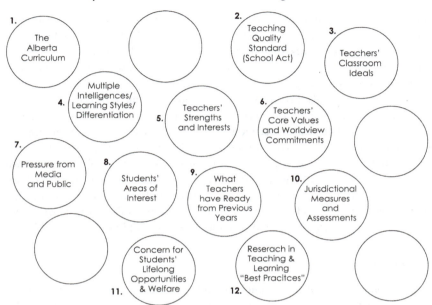

1. The Alberta Curriculum
2. Teaching Quality Standard (School Act)
3. Teachers' Classroom Ideals
4. Multiple Intelligences/ Learning Styles/ Differentiation
5. Teachers' Strengths and Interests
6. Teachers' Core Values and Worldview Commitments
7. Pressure from Media and Public
8. Students' Areas of Interest
9. What Teachers have Ready from Previous Years
10. Jurisdictional Measures and Assessments
11. Concern for Students' Lifelong Opportunities & Welfare
12. Reserach in Teaching & Learning "Best Pracitces"

**FIGURE 7.8** A never-failed-yet teaching strategy

## Variety and Contrast

Chapter 9 focuses in detail on the need to design instruction so that students gain the security offered by repetition and the engagement offered by variety and contrast. I note variety and contrast briefly here because, framed correctly, varied instruction can seem like a green space to students.

## A Quiet Area in the Classroom

The writer of a metaphor-laden book such as this one almost needs to announce when a section is to be read literally. This is one such section. Literally, if space permits, a quiet reading area might address the need for green space. Some classrooms have the space for a couch or two; most do not. Most primary classrooms have a carpeted area which, for students, generates its own set of expectations and routines. If every other square inch of the room seems given over to meeting the curriculum's demands, then a small, dedicated space might strike students as a place of retreat, offering some privacy as well (Chapter 8).

## Work Periods

Something in most students' psychological makeup causes them to be grateful when their teachers design a unit with work time built in and when they announce it as that. Work periods can happen in the classroom, the computer lab, the resource centre, or even outside. Students enjoy a work day more if they think that their teacher gave it to them because they requested it rather than because the teacher planned it in advance. And, on a different note, the reality of teaching is that sometimes we are not ready to teach a given class, especially a class that falls after lunch (that we had meant to get ready during the break). Of course, as a teacher you should never admit to students that you are unprepared. However, it is possible to embrace that occasional reality and to transform it into something beneficial for both teacher and students. You can always write on the board an assignment or activity that you thought of on the spur of the moment, and then give students the choice of work time or doing that assignment or activity. Presto, it's a green space—and you look flexible.

## Conclusion

In his book on town planning, Gibberd complains about growth where there is no "urban fence" (1967, p. 30), no barrier where development actually ends, and countryside actually starts. The two become mixed in ways that do not really protect the countryside from encroachment, and do not really liberate nearby urban dwellers to view the green space as parkland. Likewise, green space in the classroom cannot be arbitrary or haphazard. If it is, students will get confused as to what to expect on a given day, and they will not get proper respite in the green space that is offered to them. In class, when the work of learning is not demarcated clearly from breathing space, students may never really be sure they are free to breathe, and they may not become convinced that learning is the main purpose of being in class.

## References

Alexander, C., Ishikawa, S., Silverstein, M., Jacobson, M., Fiksdahl-King, I., & Angel, S. (1977). *A pattern language: Towns, buildings, construction*. New York: Oxford University Press.

Burns, G. (2005). *Waydowntown*. Canada: Burns Films/Homevision.

Gibberd, F. (1967). *Town design* (5th ed.). New York: Praeger.

Montessori, M. (1912). *The Montessori method: Scientific pedagogy as applied to child education in "the children's houses."* (A. E. George, Trans.). New York: Frederick A. Stokes.

Parrish, P. E. (2008). Plotting a learning experience. In L. Borruri & T. Stubbs (Eds.), *Handbook of visual languages for instructional design: Theories and practices* (pp. 91–111). Hershey, PA: Information Science Reference.

Parrish, P. E. (2009). Aesthetic principles for instructional design. *Educational Technology Research and Development*, 57(4), 511–528.

**FIGURE 8.1** Colonnade offers privacy with a view out to the public

# 8

# PUBLIC AND PRIVATE

The distinction between public and private runs deep in our language and in our thinking. We recognize that the two concepts represent directions on a continuum rather than hardened categories. Alexander refers to this continuum as degrees of publicness (1979, p. 127). After all, a coffee shop with a dozen people quietly working qualifies as public but has a completely different character from a stadium filled with sports fans. The unwritten (and written) expectations regarding how we behave in the two settings differ as well, even though both clearly qualify as public places. The concept of privacy likewise ranges from a group of four or five gathered at a single picnic site in a public park to a private apartment occupied by one tenant. Even that tenant is not at the end of the continuum; we could also think of the hermit in the forest who wants to get away from civilization. The ways we nuance these concepts in ordinary language indicate the importance we place on privacy. The corollary of that claim may also be true: we go to extraordinary lengths to produce great public spaces, whether they be plazas in the cathedral square, parks in front of city hall, concert venues, or stadiums.

This chapter explores some of the implications of these ideas for classrooms and the work we do in them. The literal sense of *privacy* in classrooms interests me. Is there a physical space where students can be alone when they need to be? However, I am more interested in the curricular spaces where students might find privacy. At the end of the chapter I return to the concept of public because, although much of what we do instructionally must be common to all our students, the word *public* also carries connotations of civic celebration, and I want to ask how we might incorporate more such civic life into our life together in classrooms.

## A Teaching Challenge in its Context

In most classrooms, teachers need to teach between 25 and 30 students, often more, sometimes less. They need to help those students move ahead in their learning. Normally, school boards, parents, the wider public, and teachers themselves expect a year's progress in a year. Educators know that this normal expectation is, for some students, an unreachable ideal, while others easily progress at the expected speed. To my point in this chapter, except in cases of private tutoring, such as in Rousseau's (fictional) 1762 story, *ÉMILE*, the economics of education dictate that teachers deal with large groups of students. As much as we might wish to give individualized guidance to students, we must teach them in classes. And classes are public places where many learning activities are, of necessity, common to most students.

Both my thesis and the main metaphor in this chapter are simple: just as we need private spaces in cities, buildings, and homes where so much space is public, students need curricular space—time and opportunities—to explore on their own in school settings where so much curriculum material and instruction are common to their whole class. Educational economics and instructional efficiency may dictate that we teach whole classes, but human psychology, individual differences, and the need for individual identity require that students be able to fashion some work of their own. Throughout this chapter, I will use the word *private* to denote individual assignments and work that individual students choose as well the overall routes through the unit that individual students end up following when they make a succession of choices about particular assignments.

## A Parallel Problem in Design

Town and city planning departments must consider many factors when deciding whether to grant or withhold a building permit. One of the constraints within which they work relates to the mix of private and public space. What obligations do developers have to provide public space near their buildings? How do landlords achieve the balance between private spaces that produce direct rental revenue and public spaces such as lobbies and outdoor plazas that produce no direct revenue? How do planning departments satisfy the city's budget office that they are encouraging developers to include lots of space that produces tax revenue. Buried near the bottom of the list of concerns for the planning department, but closer to the top for developers, is that individuals have spaces of their own.

Developers of office space, landlords, and tenants all must attend to the simple truth that while office workers need to collaborate and communicate, they also need privacy. Planners of retail spaces need to ensure that employees have lunchrooms, washrooms, and spaces to rest. And, of course, designers and builders of residential buildings pay a great deal of attention to how much private space is available. In short, people need privacy, and those planning the physical spaces we use must design those spaces to ensure that we get the privacy we need. Figure 8.2 illustrates what many contemporary workers consider an appalling way to provide privacy in an office setting: the cubicle. This figure also represents a frightful kind of repetition (Chapter 9). Those concerns notwithstanding, cubicles symbolize the reality that some who run businesses may maximize their use of floor space and shift the human costs of crowding onto their workers.

Many writers before me have treated the need for privacy and the tension in design and planning between private and public space (Chermayeff & Alexander, 1963; Gehl, 1987; Glazer, 1987; Rossi, 1982; Sykes, 1986). American novelist and designer Edith Wharton wrote at some length about the public/private functions of gardens in Italian estates and the private spaces in homes, even noting how the main stairway in larger homes served as both real and symbolic separation between the public spaces downstairs and the family's private spaces upstairs (Wharton, 1897, 1904). She also noted that the gala room or ballroom in the grand home functioned not only as a public space or a place for gathering. It also it served as a place of genuine celebration. Films such as *Downton Abbey* and the BBC/A&E production of *Pride and Prejudice* may help 21st-century people such as ourselves to grasp the significance of these spaces. Wharton's comments on the gala room could remind educators that those public parts of a

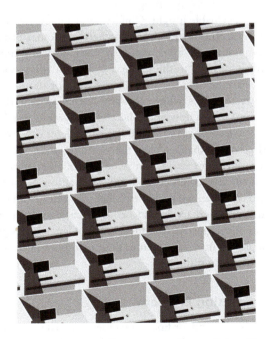

**FIGURE 8.2** A bleak representation of how some who work in office cubicles feel about the state of their work privacy

unit—the curriculum and instruction common to all students—need not be pedestrian, an idea I return to late in the chapter. This chapter is neither the first word on public and private, nor will it be the last. For a comprehensive and readable discussion of the ways we understand public and private spaces in our homes and cities, I recommend Barrie Greenbie's *Spaces: Dimensions of the Human Landscape* (1981). He treats the history and function not only of parks and public spaces, but of residential fences, side yards, back yards, and even the psychology of the single-family home. Abbreviated discussions of the concepts and how they interact appear in Alexander's *A Pattern Language*, the original inspiration for the ideas in this chapter (1977, pp. 192–196, 610–613).

A contemporary and less serious treatment of the need for privacy appeared in our own century as *Manspace: A Primal Guide to Marking Your Territory* (Martin, 2006). Martin begins with the premise that men need to carve out their own space in which to keep their collections, tinker with their toys, celebrate with their friends, or simply be alone. The book does not read as misogynist, or anti-marriage, or anti-children; it simply asserts that men need a place where they can spend their time, organize their own things, and look out (through the garage doors, a contemporary equivalent of the colonnade). To keep the focus here on unit design, I will not launch into a literary or sociological analysis of *Manspace*, but I will note that even to the end of the final page I was unable to discern whether its author was smirking throughout.

*Manspace* leads to a valuable insight. Children and adolescents and women also need their own spaces. And it strikes me that here is another place to anticipate my metaphorical question: is there room in each student's timetable, in the outline of the course, or even in the physical classroom where that student feels that some specific space belongs to him or her? I will not attempt here to address the question of private spaces within the physical classroom. But to focus on curriculum, I do want to ask how and where we as teachers might create places in our assignment and assessment structure so that students can fashion spaces that are uniquely and privately theirs within the overall course, which is obviously more of a public space. Can we design enough flexibility into our assessment structure that students can conduct in-depth exploration of an issue in which they have great interest? Can we build flexibility into our grading schema so that students can read supplementary fiction or non-fiction and get credit for it, as long as it matches the objectives of the course? Can we design so that our students all find a place where, like men in their manspaces, they can spend their time and organize their own things?

## Solutions to the Design Problem

Architects, city planners, and ordinary members of ordinary families have all found ways to address the need for privacy. The window seat serves as a ready example. To get a window seat, some friends of mine added a bay window to a sitting room adjacent to their kitchen (Figure 8.3). This room faces onto their back yard and offers views out to a small public playground and park. For reasons psychologists and designers understand better than the rest of us, perhaps related to being enclosed on three sides, most people find that the built-in window seat offers a kind of homey comfort. It feels private, even though it opens to the room.

Another example of the partial enclosure is the reading nook. Figure 8.4 shows a reading nook adjacent to a child's bedroom, built in the space above

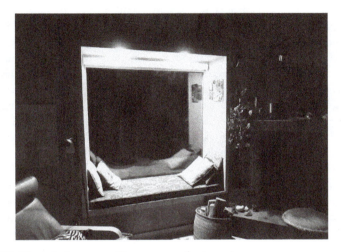

**FIGURE 8.3** The window seat offers a sense of privacy

**FIGURE 8.4** The reading nook: a place of one's own

a basement staircase. It has room for one adult and one child to read together. Given the size of the nook, the adult's legs will necessarily be bent. But the nook's small size actually increases the sense of enclosure and privacy; three people simply will not fit. Additionally, in contemporary western homes, the bedroom is already a private place, implying that this space is, in some sense, doubly private. With reference to Chapter 5's concern for entrances, let me note my awareness that the photo shows no way for a child to get up to this nook. Because the child's parents want my grandson to reach age five, at the time of writing this chapter, I had not yet built the ladder. Alexander's lyrical treatment of child caves and secret places will inspire some readers to build a nook for themselves, and will inspire nearly all readers to take more time to read, even if not in a private place (1977, pp. 927–931).

Porches and colonnades offer another example of privacy, although most architects view these two structures as transitional spaces between the public and the private. The person sitting on a porch or under a colonnade has a view of the public space outside and can be seen by passersby. But the psychology of both the porch and the colonnade works in favor of the person sitting on or under it; they feel a degree of privacy or security not available to someone simply sitting in front of a building. I will note later that group-work in classes functions as a kind of mediating space akin to the porch or colonnade.

The colonnade warrants further comment here, in part because it all but disappeared in the 20th-century but has reappeared in our own. Its beauty and, more to my point, its psychology, run deep in our souls. We love how the colonnade offers protection from the sun or the rain while still offering a view to the adjacent open space, whether that be the cloister in a monastery or the square in front of city hall. I noted in the previous paragraph that those walking or sitting under a colonnade gain a sense of security and privacy. In my city, architects have taken advantage of the psychological affordances of the colonnade and exported them to the most mundane of structures, the parking garage (Figure 8.6). I drove past the car park in that photograph for three years before learning its purpose. Prior to learning its identity, I had assumed it was a low-rise medical

"to look in a book is usually a private and intimate experience"
*Wood, Ink and Paper*, Gerard Brender à Brandis, p. 10

"every corner in a house, every angle in a room, every inch of secluded space in which we like to hide, or withdraw into ourselves, is a symbol of solitude for the imagination; that is to say, it is the germ of a room, or of a house"
*The Poetics of Space*, Gaston Bachelard, p. 136

**FIGURE 8.5** The colonnade is a transition space between public and private

**FIGURE 8.6** The façade of a parking garage improves with colonnades

or professional building. In one go, my error demonstrates both the power of the colonnade and the deep human love for privacy.

Turning our attention to private residences, in many families, individuals have their own bedrooms, another form of private space, in this case, usually private space with doors that close. On the other hand, many share their spaces at home with one or more other family and even extended-family members, rendering that space semi-private or not at all private. The current shape of the typical residential yard also illuminates our understanding of private spaces. On a typical residential street, houses have a front yard or garden visible to passersby. The space on one or both sides of a detached home will have a gate toward the front or the back of the dwelling. If the gate is located toward the front, then the side yard seems more private. Wherever the gate is—if there is one—the back yard is considered private. Most homeowners do not take offence when the children from next door need to enter the backyard to retrieve a ball or toy. But most do take offence when a total stranger comes into the back yard uninvited. Such is our sense of privacy. And such is our need for privacy. In short, we need places that belong to us alone, or, short of ownership, that we alone may use. Architects, planners, designers, and ordinary people have all addressed that need, producing many kinds of private spaces.

## Solutions in Instruction and Classrooms

How do we realize the ideas of private and public in curriculum and instruction? As I noted in the introduction to the chapter, the default mode for our classroom work is public. That results from economic necessities that are not at issue in this volume. And given that common instruction and common assessments are the main mode in which we work, I do not give much space to them here. But I do want to ask about how to carve out more private curricular space for our students.

Educational privacy is not a stand-alone principle. It obviously connects to the idea of places to breathe or green spaces (in Chapter 7). If, as a student, I am strongly motivated about completing a project related to the earth's place in the solar system (Arizona, grade 6)—that my teacher allowed me to choose—then working on that project will seem less like school work to me. I *get* to do that instead of *having* to do that. The idea of entrances from Chapter 5 also connects here. To stick with the solar system example, if the earth's place in the solar system has fascinated me for years, then as an Arizona sixth-grader, my teacher's having permitted me to go into depth on this topic may serve as a kind of invitation or entrance to my whole science course and perhaps even my whole school year. Giving students a measure of choice about some assignments allows them to build variety into the course (Chapter 9) and allowing them to do so in each unit can function as a predictable, constant element of the course (Chapter 9: Repetition and Variety), offering coherence (Chapter 6).

What strategies can teachers use in unit design to address students' need for private or semi-private places? My first offering as a solution is conceptual. That is, that we not view instruction and learning activities common to all the students in a room as a problem; I do not at all want to frame this section of the chapter as "public is bad, private is good." Classes, students, and teachers all need both.

As I noted earlier with regard to Edith Wharton, public spaces can be places of celebration and joy. I will end the chapter by returning to that idea. First, I will deal with what some have called a place of one's own, those areas of learning and assessment that students are able to carve out as a kind of private learning domain. Then I will treat what sociologists call mediating structures, the means by which individuals can participate in society without having to interact with all of society, that is, clubs, religious organizations, community groups, voluntary settings where individuals join with other individuals in some common cause or interest. Metaphorically, these structures may recall the colonnade or porch. Finally, I will return to the concept of the public, attempting to shed light on common classroom activities from a perspective of civic celebration.

## The Private: A Place of One's Own

All students should be able to identify spaces in a course that, in their view, actually belong to them, spaces where they can complete work being done by none—or at least very few—of their classmates. Can each student feel that certain elements of the course belong only to him or her, that no one else reported on this topic, completed this assignment, researched this mammal, read this article, or took this viewpoint? This should be true in every unit of a course, perhaps even every instructional day. This claim has significant implications for both instruction and assessment, and I want to dedicate a significant part of this section to suggested ways of meet this condition.

All my readers will be familiar with the work on learning styles that began with David Kolb (1984) or with the idea of multiple intelligences and the name Howard Gardner (1983, 1999). Many readers will know some of the details of both these approaches to individual differences and perhaps even some of the literature that compares and attempts to reconcile the two. I mention this work as one approach to framing my argument that students need places of their own. In my lists of possible contents for layers, I include attention to learning styles and multiple intelligences. Students need to be reminded periodically that no one else in the school has their unique combination of strengths and interests. And we need to build into our term plans spaces within which students can play to the strengths they bring. Related to those matters, as teachers wondering about privacy in classroom settings, we should note the number of students in our classrooms who have been identified with a learning disability or as talented and gifted and placed on an individual learning plan. When educators plan accommodations and adaptations for such students, they are, in effect, offering a place of one's own, a private garden patio akin to the one shown in Figure 8.7.

Some teachers require that in each unit all students complete a set of common assignments but have the freedom to choose some other assignments. That freedom could be limited to three or four suggested topics listed in a unit outline or it could be wide open. Especially with secondary students, teachers can publish the learning outcomes for the unit and give students the freedom to devise their own projects, requiring that students submit a one-page proposal before launching the full project. The suggestion to offer wide choice comes with a codicil. The teacher's job remains to point to the centre (Chapter 3) and to maintain the boundaries (Chapter 4). We have all had the student for whom a curriculum of all dinosaurs, or all hobbits, or all Fibonacci sequences all the time would seem just perfect. Those students are part of the reason we need to provide boundaries and make clear where those boundaries lie. Thus, the claim that we need to provide private spaces is constrained by the standards of the jurisdiction within which we work. Dinosaurs or hobbits might offer a high level of engagement or curricular coherence (Chapter 6) to one student, but as responsible educators, we suspect that coherence would ultimately come at a significant cost to that student.

I offer here a permitted example from a secondary teacher who classifies all the assignments in every unit into either *Basket 1* or *Basket 2*. Basket 1 includes those assignments and assessments required of every student in the class. The assignments and their due dates are listed in the unit outline distributed on the first day of the unit. In a typical unit in this class, roughly half the grades are based on the work in Basket 1. Every unit also includes Basket 2 readings, assignments, and assessments. The unit outlines always include a few suggested Basket 2 assignments worth enough grades for students to choose work in formats where they can show more strength or work on topics that interest them. Students also get to propose and complete assignments of their own devising and submit them as part of Basket 2. Basket 1 and Basket 2 are a way to recognize the public and the private.

Mihaly Csikszentmihalyi's decades of research on flow and the conditions likely to induce it are a great way to draw this discussion of private spaces to a

**FIGURE 8.7**  The enclosed patio, a paradigm of privacy

---

## ARCHITECTS, WORK SPACES, AND COMMON WORK

In "Toward a Personal Workplace," Christopher Alexander and several colleagues explain their concern that designers of workspaces produce environments where people actually want to be "in the same sense that [they] want to curl up in a corner with a pillow on a Saturday afternoon" (1987, p. 130). Part of their argument raises an interesting question for curriculum and instruction. They argue that people's mental images of ideal workplaces contain archetypal elements such as desks. They describe the archetypal desk as one full of deskness (p. 133), and they immediately note that despite their odd choice of language, the psychological aspect for the office worker is quite real; he or she will experience dissonance if asked to work on a flat surface hung from the side of a cubicle.

One question the idea of archetypes may raise for educators is how students unpack the concepts of *assignment* or *schoolwork*. If those two terms ordinarily bring to students' minds images of a complete lack of choice or of meaningless work, what kind of (good) dissonance will choice about their assignments possibly induce? On the other hand, if they have become accustomed to choosing real work for a real audience in the real world what kind of disappointment will they experience if they have no choice and all their work is boring and common? By common, I mean in both senses: the whole class does the same thing, and it is ordinary.

---

close (1982, 1990, 1997, 2000, 2002). His criteria for flow include loss of self-awareness, loss of sense of the passage of time, complete absorption in the task at hand, and a view that the rewards of the activity are inherent rather than external (the list varies from book to book, but these four appear regularly). One example of a private activity in a classroom is Sustained Silent Reading. Teachers who regularly incorporate sustained silent reading (SSR) in their unit designs and day-to-day planning know that some students will become completely engaged in their reading within minutes of starting to read, satisfying some of Csikszentmihalyi's criteria for flow states. That students may read a book of their own choosing implies that SSR also can meet the concern for privacy.

### Groups: Mediating Structures

Social scientists designate as mediating structures those places and associations that function somewhere between the private and the whole society. Some call these structures *third places*. In fact, one Seattle bookstore has appropriated that name to indicate its wish to serve its community as a mediating space, situated between private life and the individual's connections to work, government, and society as a whole. Classrooms need third places as well, and for many teachers, group work is that place that requires conversation with others but offers safety to the individual. Because my readers are intimately familiar with how to use groups, and because a vast research literature on using groups already exists, I offer only very brief comments in this section.

Groups meet the need for students to identify with some smaller structure than the whole classroom. For the sake of argument, say that out of thirty students, roughly twenty in any class will begin the term with some friends in the class already. Whether from their neighbourhood, from sports or music, from another class or year in school, or from some other affiliation outside of school, two-thirds already have someone they know and can feel comfortable near. The other third of students in that class need a smaller community of people. They need to be members of a group that regularly meets. In those classes where teachers maintain the composition of breakout groups constant over a month, a unit or a year, that smaller community could be the break-out group. Other times, for example in Think-Pair-Share, it may simply be the people seated closest. In whatever ways the teacher initiates or structures this, students need an association with a body of persons smaller than the whole class. The inclusion of physical breakout spaces in newer school buildings shows wider recognition in our own time for privacy, an encouraging sign.

Without packing this short section with ideas, I have suggested that groups have a more important function that we often recognize in the busy-ness of carrying out our day-to-day classroom programs. The importance of groups lies in part in their being venues in that space between public and private.

**FIGURE 8.8** Group work in class combines private and public

## The Public as Civic Celebration

I close this chapter by returning to the concept of the public and calling for us all to find ways to make our common assignments and assessments uncommon. Can we make the public aspect of classroom work into something special, not simply a default mode dictated by economics?

Late in his book, *Crossing the Post-Modern Divide* (1992), Albert Borgmann includes a wonderful essay about civic celebration, one consistent with the short passage about the street I quoted from Philip Johnson in Chapter 6 and with Edith Wharton's comments about the gala room that I noted earlier in this chapter. In Borgmann's vision of the city, people gather simply for the joy of being together and seeing each other. And they gather to celebrate national independence, sports and electoral wins, religious events, and Earth Day. I grant that classroom economies of scale dictate that we frequently require that most of our students join in the same activities and complete the same assignments. But in my vision of the classroom, consistent with Johnson's conception of the street and Borgmann's vision of the city, some of the common activities become celebrations of our students' idiomatic interests and unique abilities. The project or poster exhibition becomes a classroom's civic celebration, with the same mood that we expect to prevail at a festival. If the 33,000,000 records returned from a quick search of *classroom celebrations* indicate anything about teachers' creativity, this idea lies within our reach. We need to do this for our students.

And we need to do it for ourselves. The days when teachers say, "You know, I could do this for free," are often the days when we give students opportunities to show their best work. This may be more the case if the work they present is real work for a real audience in the real world. Let us build and celebrate the public aspects of our classroom work so we and our students have the pleasure of more of those days.

## References

Alexander, C. (1979). *The timeless way of building.* New York: Oxford University Press.

Alexander, C., Anninou, A., Black, G., & Rheinfrank, J. (1987). Toward a personal workplace. *Architectural Record, 175*(9), 130–141.

Alexander, C., Ishikawa, S., Silverstein, M., Jacobson, M., Fiksdahl-King, I., & Angel, S. (1977). *A pattern language: Towns, buildings, construction.* New York: Oxford University Press.

Bachelard, G. (1964). *The poetics of space* (M. Jolas, Trans.). Boston, MA: Beacon.

Borgmann, A. (1992). *Crossing the postmodern divide.* Chicago, IL: University of Chicago Press.

Brender à Brandis, G. (1980). *Wood, ink and paper.* Erin, ON: The Porcupine's Quill.

Chermayeff, S., & Alexander, C. (1963). *Community and privacy: Toward a new architecture of humanism.* New York: Doubleday/Anchor.

Csikszentmihalyi, M. (1982). Intrinsic motivation and effective teaching: A flow analysis. In J. L. Bess (Ed.), *Motivating professors to teach effectively* (pp. 15–26). San Francisco, CA: Jossey-Bass.

Csikszentmihalyi, M. (1990). *Flow: The psychology of optimal experience.* New York: Harper and Row.

Csikszentmihalyi, M. (1997). *Finding flow: The psychology of engagement with everyday life.* New York: Harper-Collins.

Csikszentmihalyi, M. (2000). Education for the 21st century. *Education Week*, 19(32), 64–66.

Csikszentmihalyi, M. (2002). *Motivating people to learn.* Retrieved from www.edutopia.org/mihaly-csikszentmihalyi-motivating-people-learn.

Gardner, H. (1983). *Frames of mind: The theory of multiple intelligences.* New York: Basic.

Gardner, H. (1999). *Intelligence reframed: Multiple intelligences for the 21st century.* New York: Basic Books.

Gehl, J. (1987). *Life between buildings: Using public space.* New York: Van Nostrand Reinhold.

Glazer, N. (1987). *The public face of architecture: civic culture and public spaces.* New York: Collier Macmillan/Free Press.

Greenbie, B. B. (1981). *Spaces: Dimensions of the human landscape.* New Haven, CT: Yale University Press.

Kolb, D. A. (1984). *Experiential learning: Experience as the source of learning and development.* Englewood Cliffs, NJ: Prentice Hall.

Martin, S. (2006). *Manspace: A primal guide to marking your territory.* Newtown, CT: Taunton.

Rossi, A. (1982). *The architecture of the city.* Boston, MA: MIT Press.

Sykes, C. S. (1986). *Private palaces: Life in the great London houses.* New York: Viking.

Wharton, E. (1897). *The decoration of houses.* New York: Norton.

Wharton, E. (1904). *Italian villas and their gardens.* Boston, MA: Da Capo/Hachette.

**FIGURE 8.9** The public at its best: civic life in the plaza

**FIGURE 9.1** Variety and repetition

# 9
# REPETITION AND VARIETY

Every educator faces the challenge of how to balance repetition and variety. I will argue in this chapter that teachers need to keep many larger structures and routines consistent because students find safety in predictability. I note as well that threads and layers offer not only the coherence and connection I noted in Chapter 6, but they also constitute a healthy form of repetition that offers a measure of security to students who, justifiably, wonder each day what school will hold. The dual corollary argument of course is that students and (most) teachers get bored without variety, but that variety should not be endless. My use of the word *challenge* in the first sentence of this paragraph is thus not unreflective; finding the space between stultifying repetition and life-simplifying repetition is indeed a challenge. Finding the balance between life-giving variety and head-spinning variety is also a challenge. Educators must address both challenges at once. We might wish we could tackle these challenges consecutively, but their component parts come to us simultaneously, and like puzzlers completing two different puzzles from a single pile of pieces, we must do both at once.

In this chapter, I follow the lead of the authors of many art and design instruction books who tie these concepts together in a single chapter. I treat them together here because in unit design these elements connect to each other, and when they are incorporated into a unit design in the right mix, they increase student efficacy and engagement, and therefore learning.

Most students need predictability and structure to succeed. Their work environment needs to be both free and ordered. To use a metaphor, the student in the class where the teacher does the same thing day after day may experience that class the way I experienced the neighbourhood I grew up in Regina, Saskatchewan. In (my first) 18 years of life in that grid, I never got lost. Even at five years of age, I knew the way home from school. Neighborhood locals always knew that addresses in the 900 block were between 3rd and 4th Avenue (yes, that part could have been simpler). My point is that the grid was simple and predictable, and its simplicity and predictability made some parts of life easier. Not being a town planner, I will leave the conversation about the advantages and disadvantages of grid-planning to experts; as an educator I can see how the educational equivalent of grid-planning benefits both students and teachers, while at the same time I do not believe that repetition should be seen as an educational good without conditions.

Repetition pairs nicely with variety, although we sometimes forget that our students need both. Graduating teachers have heard a thousand times that they must employ a variety of learning and teaching strategies or students will become bored and disengaged. I do not question the truth of this claim, and I doubt that many of my readers do, either. I experienced that boredom myself as a student; in fact, I even had to repeat a grade 12 course because the teacher was so boring I completely disengaged from the class the first time around. Many of my readers will have seen the look on students' faces that says something like, "Seriously, are we doing that again? I'd rather have dental work without freezing." Most educators know the look; it is the pedagogical equivalent of a Soviet-era apartment block. In short, I take no issue with the assertion that we and our students need variety. As you will see as we work through the chapter, however, I do want to add some conditions to the claim.

The words *contrast* and *unity* do not appear in the chapter title, but both concepts connect to this chapter. While the concepts of repetition and variety are semantically related but quite separate, contrast and variety are more like semantic cousins inasmuch as they overlap significantly in meaning. One might distinguish them by noting that in unit design *variety* might imply using a number of different strategies or altering the contents regularly, where *contrast* might

**FIGURE 9.2** The arches in this colonnade repeat. The furnishings vary

imply using strategies and contents that differ markedly from each other. For the purposes of this chapter, the distinction between the two does not need to be especially sharp, and I will use the two terms somewhat interchangeably throughout the chapter.

The word *unity* connects to the above three concepts. Many who write about art, aesthetics, design, and architecture argue that unity is achieved through the right combination of repetition and variety. They argue that contrast does not diminish unity, a thesis borne out by Figure 9.1 on the opening page of this chapter. The word *unity* is often called into service when the word *coherence* is being defined, and vice versa. As I treat it here, unity connects back to Chapter 5's discussion of coherence. But I raise the matter here again because it connects to contrast, which is intimately linked to variety. As I noted in Chapter 5, the educator wanting to increase coherence and unity can look to the curriculum itself (assuming it is conceived and constructed well), to consistency in classroom routines and practices, and to built-in consistent instructional practices. Unity and contrast may appear equally as paradoxical a pairing as variety and repetition. And not to make too much of etymology, but a unit should have unity.

## Repetition

This discussion of repetition focuses first on some the difficulties of repetition before it turns to life-giving repetition. In my introductory remarks above, I mentioned the street plan grid in the neighbourhood where I grew up, and I claimed that the grid offered efficiencies. It did so in transport and navigation, in infrastructure costs, and even in the speed at which I could deliver newspapers on my paper route. But the navigational simplicity that the grid street plan offered was offset by a kind of tedium. Every city block was the same size (300'

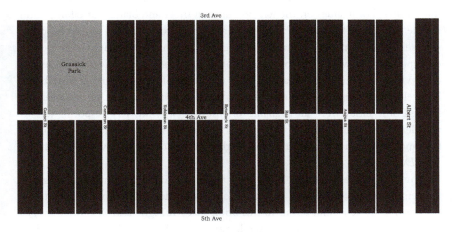

**FIGURE 9.3** Grid layout of the author's childhood neighborhood

× 500' including the width of the back lane and one adjacent street). Every lot was either 25, 37.5 or 50 feet wide. On Cameron Street, where I delivered newspapers for three years, I knew how many steps to take between every house on my route. On a dare, I once attempted to deliver to all the houses on one block with my eyes closed. That did not turn out as I expected, although it did add variety. Furthermore, it caused me again to notice things that years of repetition had led me to ignore. Switching back to the metaphor, all students benefit from structure and predictability. Some students actually flourish if every class has the same structure. But a majority of students need variety. In classrooms, repetition is not by itself an unmitigated good. Repeated elements are necessary to the success of a classroom program. But too much repetition will diminish students' energy for learning.

At some point all of us have been trapped in a class where students literally did the same kind of work every day. In the bleak (and aging) American film, *Teachers*, a secondary teacher nicknamed "Ditto" uses worksheets in every class, every day. His planning calendar likely looked like the image in Figure 9.4. As his classes enter his room each day, the students from the front desk in each row pick up stacks of photo-copied worksheets and distribute them to their rows. When the closing bell rings, the students leave their worksheets on Ditto's desk as they exit the room. During class, Ditto reads the newspaper and snoozes intermittently. The most bleakly comic moment in the film has Ditto die during class and no one know he has done so until he fails to appear in the staff lounge at the end of the school day.

Of course, no teacher would ever admit to being as boring as Ditto. But I have had students tell me about courses where every class consists of a deck of PowerPoint slides, supplied by the textbook's publisher and linked with deadly precision to the textbook, accompanied by handout sheets with thumbnails of three PowerPoint slides on the left side of each sheet and blanks for taking notes on the right side. If the film *Teachers* were remade today, Ditto would be using precisely that format, confirming the claim of unknown origin that power corrupts, and PowerPoint corrupts absolutely. In her description of a specific class where the professor "teaches" this way, one of my students reported that he welcomed them not to attend class if they preferred not to because the PowerPoint slides were all available on the course wiki. My response was to wonder about that professor's salary. Surely the university could hire a student for much less than a professor's salary if the only teaching task were to push the *Page Down* key.

The film character Ditto is an easy target for anyone wanting to flag the dangers of repetition. Other forms of repetition, closer to home, warrant our attention. I say at several points in this book that McTighe and Wiggins brought needed focus to the order in which educators thought about instruction. In fact, we should start by asking what it is we want students to know rather than what it is we want to teach (or worse, what we taught last year). But some students and some teachers experience big-questions fatigue. Both would like to organize lessons in other ways. In schools that have moved toward enquiry learning, some students experience what one colleague calls *enquiry fatigue*; they get tired of being the ones who always have to identify the big questions. I will not attempt here to speak for the advocates of backwards-by-design, but I suspect that many of them would concede that backwards-by-design should never be boring and that teachers must vary the teaching and learning strategies even as they remain constant in their foundational understanding of how instruction works best.

Having laid out the negative effects of unmitigated repetition, I now want to defend repetition in the name of student learning power and even beauty. I start with beauty, and very simply, with an image described by aesthetics philosopher, Panayotis Michelis. He asks us to imagine two pillars standing near each other. On his account, as we imagine them we immediately sense a rhythm, one connected to one of the most basic patterns in our visual vocabulary. He writes that "we feel a peculiar pleasure, as when we see a row of trees in a meadow, or animals following each other in a field. Here it is not only the victory of the erection of a pillar, which is satisfactory in itself, but also the victory of order, which we can sense everywhere and which we seek everywhere" (1977, p. 221). Viewing two standing pillars as the victory of order may be more than some will grant, but Michelis does help us see how deep the need for repetition may run in the human soul.

Over half a century ago, Bruner offered the idea of the spiral curriculum (1960). In this design, students circle back to what they have studied before, each

| Sun | Mon | Tue | Wed | Thu | Fri | Sat |
|---|---|---|---|---|---|---|
| | Work sheets<br>Work time | Work sheets<br>Work time | Work sheets<br>Work time | Work sheets<br>Work time | Work sheets<br>Work time | |
| | Work sheets<br>Work time | Work sheets<br>Work time | Work sheets<br>Work time | Work sheets<br>Work time | Work sheets<br>Work time | |
| | Work sheets<br>Work time | Work sheets<br>Work time | Work sheets<br>Work time | Work sheets<br>Work time | Work sheets<br>Work time | |

**FIGURE 9.4** The planning sheet of a teacher whose classes students advise each other to avoid

time with more critical questions and more conceptual tools with which to approach those questions. In Bruner's vision, they come back with more ability to self-reflect and to engage in discourse with others, including people with whom they do not agree. Much K-12 curriculum follows Bruner's advice: students encounter the weights and measures unit in primary school and again in senior high; they study Greece as an example of democratic government in middle school and again in senior high. As teachers know, inevitably, early in a unit related to something students have studied three or four years earlier, a student will blurt out something along the lines of, "We already took this in fifth grade!" (That this same student may have watched several movies two dozen times does not seem inconsistent with that complaint, indicating room for further development in the self-reflection dimension.) Although we likely would not use the word *recursion* with primary pupils, we may want to explain early and often that we can learn more each time we come back around to a topic. That kind of repetition is healthy. Teachers have invented a thousand ways to use repetition effectively in classroom work. Some repeat a specific class activity or kind of assignment once in each unit. Some elements loop through the course or unit at a higher frequency than that, others at a lower frequency, not even appearing in every unit in the school year.

In Chapter 6, I introduced the twin ideas of threads and layers as means of building more coherence in a course. For simplicity, I will repeat my stipulated definitions. Threads are activities or topics we give two to three minutes to two or three times per week, for example, a mathematics thread where we track today's weather in relation to long-term seasonal averages. Layers take five to ten minutes per day and we use them four or five times per week. The daily weather could serve as an example of a layer if the teacher included tracking the day's

**FIGURE 9.5**
Andy Goldsworthy's Storm King Wall, near Windsor, New York, mixes repetition and variety

**FIGURE 9.6**
Repetition, variety, and contrast contribute to unity and move the viewer's eyes toward the centre

weather in several other locations, or having students carry out more complicated calculations. As a layer, this particular example becomes interdisciplinary, entailing science, geography, and mathematics. Repetition in the form of layers and threads yields a kind of continuity (Chapter 6: Coherence and Connections) or even security to students. Lots of things at school change from day to day and week to week, but we track the weather consistently. As a thread or layer, tracking the weather would interest students for several weeks, but (except for a tiny minority) certainly not for the whole year.

## Variety

In the summary of this chapter in Chapter 2, I made reference to the proverb that variety is the spice of life, and then immediately added the note that it is the spice, not the main course. I have argued in this chapter that repetition is necessary, but too much repetition causes boredom. The parallel to that claim applies to variety. What I call head-spinning variety undermines students' need for predictability and security and ultimately may diminish their learning powers. Fully aware that the word *balance* suffers from overuse, I nevertheless want to argue that we need to find the balance between too much variety and too little.

To recall my discussion of street-grid planning from earlier in this chapter, town planners who use the grid know of its advantages. Street naming and numbering are simplified so that people can find an address easily. Infrastructure costs are lower. Because land use is efficient, more people can live in less space. But the grid layout creates its own problems, one of which relates quite clearly to curriculum and another that perhaps does not. The problem most clearly related to curriculum arises out of the similarity of every block in a grid. Everything tends to look the same. Boredom and even a kind of blindness set in as students (and perhaps teachers) begin to function on autopilot. The course which is divided perfectly into sections where every section contains the same material (for example, discussion day after day or lecture day after day) creates the same kind of boredom that the grid layout can create in a city. To prevent such boredom from setting in, we need variety, and several ways to implement variety come to mind.

Of course, the most obvious place to work toward variety is in teaching methods, or teaching/learning strategies. Because both pre-service teachers and in-service teachers hear about the need for varied methods so often, I will give only one paragraph to it here. Most teachers draw from a repertoire of perhaps 50 favorite methods; they are likely expert at a couple dozen of these. But most teachers rely on a core repertoire of five or six methods. For example, a teacher's core repertoire might include Think-Pair-Share, having students identify what question each paragraph in a passage answers, reader's theatre, blackout poetry, agree-disagree sheet, Venn diagrams, discussion of film-clips, and table discussions.

This hypothetical teacher knows several dozen more methods, but she uses these most regularly. For the sake of argument, let me suggest that she could aim at expanding her repertoire. If she makes that her aim, she could turn to several resources, including the subject-area specialist in her school district, colleagues and pre-service teachers in her building, professors in her subject-area at the nearest university, and other experts. She can also turn to printed and online resources, such as *The Ontario Curriculum Unit Planner: Teaching Learning Companion*, an encyclopedia of strategies that I recommend again in Chapter 13 (https://faculty.nipissingu.ca/darleneb/Relevant_links_docs/telrsta2002.pdf). I want to move from possibility to something stronger by suggesting that not only does an expanded repertoire add variety to instruction and thereby make learning more interesting for both teacher and students. Regularly adding new strategies to one's repertoire is an excellent way for one to stay professionally vital into the later decades of one's career (Snowdon, 2001).

A second means of introducing variety is by varying the kinds and weights of assignments and assessments. Varying the kinds of assignments needs neither defense nor explanation here because literally thousands of books and websites offer advice relevant to that matter. But a couple comments are in order. A mix of teacher-defined questions and student-generated, enquiry-type questions brings variety. In the category of teacher-defined questions, we can get variety by including a range from easy to difficult to nearly-impossible to answer. In one textbook project I worked on, we provided three levels of questions, called

**FIGURE 9.7** A canal in Hamburg showing repetition and variety

Checkpoint, Reflection, and Brain Freeze. Questions in the last category were meant to slow students down or to generate deep discussion. A question like "At night when the lights are off in the gallery, what is on the walls: art, or only paintings?" adds variety in a class where students have had to master a lot of factual information. I will not say more here about varying the kinds of assignments or their levels of difficulty but will recommend the comic opening scene of Wes Anderson's 1998 film, *Rushmore*, where a math teacher challenges his secondary students to solve a problem that had allegedly vexed some of the great minds in mathematics.

Let me offer a warrant and a schema for varying the weights of assignments, by which I mean the percentage of a unit's grade attached to each assignment. In the next chapter (Chapter 10: Gradients, Harmony, and Levels of Scale), I suggest a consistent and limited scale of assignment weights. By *consistent*, I mean that it is used throughout the course. By *limited*, I mean that it does not have a vast variety of weights or points. For example, throughout a school year, all assignments, tests, and projects are weighted at one of a limited number of points on a scale, possibly 5%, 10%, 20% and 40% (of a unit's total). Such a scale is the kind of repetition that gives students a sense of control over their work inasmuch as they both know and think they know how much a given assignment will count in their overall unit grade. Having some lower-weight work due in the first few days of a unit helps get weaker students into the learning materials and can give them the satisfaction of having some grades in the teacher's record book or spreadsheet early in the unit. Such a limited scale simplifies record-keeping for the teacher. It also serves as a design tool because it reminds the teacher that every unit needs a variety of weights, what I call in the next chapter a *balanced range of sizes*.

A third way to design variety into the unit is by means of individual and group work. Recall that in the previous chapter I argued that students need a place of their own. In every unit, every student should have the opportunity to complete at least one unique task or project (repetition). Some teachers ensure this by offering a list of perhaps ten more topics than there are students in the class. Only one student may sign up for any topic, guaranteeing variety as well as what I called in Chapter 8 a *private place*. Almost certainly, every reader of this paragraph already uses group work and whole-class instruction. In light of that, I am aware that I may be arguing here for what is already happening in classrooms. But there is something in this practice that meets the concerns of this chapter, not just the previous one.

Finally, we can introduce a great deal of variety in how we design the use of our time, from the day all the way to the year. We should divide the year into units of a variety of sizes, a claim I repeat in Chapter 10. Not on the first time through a course, but by the third time through, we will know how long each unit takes. We should plan accordingly, even if, to design in variety, we plan the course so that the units may not be in the order specified by the jurisdiction.

We can also incorporate short activities of two or three days' duration between units to add variety and offer a green space to our students and perhaps to ourselves (Chapter 7). In Chapter 13, where I offer step-by-step instructions for designing a unit according to the principles in this book, I suggest that we design in light of the likely energy levels students will bring to school at different times during the unit. Recognizing and working with these levels, an approach suggested first by Parrish (2005, 2009), will force us to design variety into our units. In light of Parrish's research, I suggest in Chapter 13 that we classify our own repertoire of strategies into three groups according to their voltage levels (and plan to use the higher-voltage strategies on days when students will bring less energy). Doing so will add variety. I also suggest in Chapter 13 that every class period should include work time. For the sake of variety, we should vary what part of the period we allocate to that work time. Students will find security in knowing that they will get desk time, and we can offer variety by scheduling it anytime in the period we want to.

## Conclusion

Used judiciously, repeated elements in a design strengthen coherence and continuity. Used judiciously, variety increases engagement. Contrast can draw attention to the centre of a design. Combined correctly, the three elements— repetition, variety, contrast—can increase unity. Across all design fields, including graphic design and architecture, these combinations of elements produce the same agreeable effects. We must begin to view instruction as a design field, and variety and repetition as elements for intentional use in design within that field. When we use variety and repetition intentionally and judiciously, we will see student engagement and efficacy increase.

## References

Bruner, J. S. (1960). *The process of education*. Cambridge, MA: Harvard University Press.

Michelis, P. A. (1977). *Aisthetikos: Essays in art, architecture, and aesthetics*. Detroit, MI: Wayne State University Press.

Parrish, P. E. (2005). Embracing the aesthetics of instructional design. *Educational Technology*, 45(2), 16–25.

Parrish, P. E. (2009). Aesthetic principles for instructional design. *Educational Technology Research and Development*, 57(4), 511–528.

Snowdon, D. (2001). *Aging with grace: The nun study*. Toronto: Bantam.

**FIGURE 9.8** A building in Rome, combining variety and repetition

**FIGURE 10.1** The Canada Life Building in Toronto uses setbacks to hide its volume

# 10

# GRADIENTS, HARMONY, AND LEVELS OF SCALE

In this chapter, I continue the argument in Chapter 9 regarding variety, although I ask here that we achieve that variety by incorporating a range of sizes of activities, assignments, and assessments in the units we design. Many designers and architects refer to this variation with the phrase *levels of scale*, and the first section in the chapter follows that heading. In the second part of the chapter, I argue the related point that we must follow the lead of website designers and ask a UX—user experience—question when thinking about unit design: how do they perceive the volume or mass of the contents they are meant to study. Our students need to perceive that the work ahead is on a human scale. This second discussion is called "Hiding the Volume," a title meant to catch this imperative. In that section, I proceed metaphorically, comparing the design of massive buildings to instructional design, and I ask that we hide some of the mass or volume of what lies ahead so our students' street view does not intimidate them and thereby diminish their own capacity to succeed with the materials.

Each of the two sections of the chapter divides into two parts. In the first part of each respective section, I explore how designers and, especially, architects deal with issues of scale. In both cases—levels of scale and human scale—those who deal professionally with these questions have offered creative solutions to the problems. In the second part of each of the two major sections, I explore ways that educators might approach the parallel educational challenge.

## Proportion and Levels of Scale in Architecture

Checking exhaustively the 24,000,000 web pages returned by searching *design principles* will reveal that almost all of them list proportion as one of the principles. Simply put, proportion has to do with the relative sizes of the various elements in a design. Almost all discussions of proportion advocate that designers include a variety of sizes in a design. They likewise argue that proportion and variety produce symmetry and harmony. In my defense of variety in Chapter 9, I argued for variation in teaching and learning strategies and assessment. In the second part of this section on proportion and levels of scale, I will argue for varied sizes of contents and grading weights.

The oldest surviving work on architecture, by Vitruvius, is an attempt to interpret Greek architectural principles for a Roman audience (Pollio, 1960). Vitruvius had a deep concern that parts be related appropriately to each other, that is, proportion and symmetry (pp. 14, 72–75, 109–113, 174–80). He calls proportion *eurythmy* and distinguishes it from symmetry (p. 14). Although he seems to ignore his distinction between proportion and symmetry later in the book, his concern for them both nevertheless runs deep, even reaching as far as the heights of columns relative to their thickness and to whether a given column is in the middle of a row or at the end. He even describes how to compensate for inaccuracies in human perception with taller columns. Regarding proportion, Vitruvius included in his prescriptions the demand that designers attend appropriately to the internal details of a building and to its setting. His language (even in translation) might seem foreign to readers today, but his ideas echo through discussions of design and architecture to our own time.

The first still-extant work on architecture after Vitruvius, *On the Art of Building in Ten Books*, appears in the mid-1400s, from Leon Battista Alberti (Alberti, 1988). He introduces proportion and scale as quickly as did Vitruvius, expressing his concern early for ". . . appropriate place, exact numbers, proper scale, and a graceful order for whole buildings and for each of their constituent parts, so that the whole form and appearance of the building may depend on the

**FIGURE 10.2** The Santa Maria Novella in Florence (1448–1470) by Leon Battista Alberti

lineaments alone" (p. 7). Not only should we design so that individual buildings have their own harmony. Alberti believed that viewers of buildings should be able to "... recognize the same lineaments in several different buildings that share one and the same form, that is, when the parts, as well as the siting and order, correspond with one another in their every line and angle" (p. 7, connected to my Chapter 6: Coherence and Connections). He continues his argument with the claim that architects should be able to conceive whole forms in the mind, by thinking only about the combination of lines and angles, before even thinking about materials. Throughout Italy, one can see many of Alberti's buildings, including his Santa Maria Novella (Figure 10.2). His expression (in this example) of the enduring design principles of proportion and symmetry does not fit contemporary sensibilities, but he nevertheless illustrates what he argued in the *Ten Books*; one can easily see the kinds of correspondence he argued for in his text.

## Proportion and Levels of Scale in Instructional Design

Having introduced the chapter by means of the written works of a classical architect and an early Renaissance architect rather than with any of the 24,000,000 online offerings, I turn now to the question of how educators might follow the lead of architects and designers by attending to proportion and levels of scale in our design of teaching units. The principle of gradients and promoting harmony through the proportional use of space applies to curriculum and course planning in some revealing and interesting ways. I offer several areas to apply the principles that Vitruvius, Alberti, and most others have prescribed for good design.

First, day-to-day classroom activities that do not figure in formal assessment of students' learning should be varied in the length of time they take to complete. This is an obvious corollary to my call in Chapter 9 that teachers vary the types of activities we use in class. In short, we vary the types and we vary the times. I suggest that we identify which of our planned classroom activities are likely to take only 10–20 minutes, which are likely to take from 40 minutes to a whole class period, and which will require several periods to complete. We should design our units and individual class days so students experience a mix, a balanced range of sizes. According to design theory, such variety actually creates harmony.

Second, we should apply the same principle to student assignments. We could start by dividing them into three groups along the lines of minor, mid-sized, and major. An obvious corollary to this kind of division is that different sizes of assignments will carry different weights in the calculation of students' grades. Some teachers actually fix assignment weights at three or four distinct levels, even adjusting the size of some assignments to fit the simplified grading schema. Out of a unit total of 100 marks, for example, all assignments are weighted at either 5%, 10%, 20% or 40%. These fixed weights help students judge the importance of each assignment, clarifying and simplifying their planning. But fixed weights also accomplish what Vitruvius and Alberti called for. If one views the façade of the Santa Maria Novella (Figure 10.2) as a metaphor, one can see that some parts are weighted at 5% each, some at 10%, one at 20% (the band above the ground floor), and one at 40% (the rectangle above the band). Furthermore, fixed weights help teachers achieve the balanced range of sizes. Few teachers today (at least not in K-12 education) would weight a summative assessment worth 80% of a unit's grade. Likewise, few would require 20 small assignments worth 5% each in a unit. By offering a formula for mixing the sizes of assignments and assessments, a fixed-weight schema with only three or four levels helps teachers simplify unit design and allows them to plan in a more agile way. This approach simplifies grading calculations for teachers and it helps students understand easily the grading structures within which we require that they work!

Having argued for variety, I want to take a contrarian view for a moment. If in most units in a course, the grading schema incorporated the design principle of a balanced range of sizes, how would students receive a unit that entailed, say, four assignments all carrying equal weight? The balanced range of assignments disappears in that one unit. But the type of grading schema is thus varied between units. The grading in every unit can obviously be structured the same way (it certainly simplifies record-keeping) but altering the structure in one unit introduces a variation that most students will welcome (Chapter 9: variety and contrast).

Veteran teachers know that each size and kind of assignment has its own strengths and weaknesses, all of which I will not catalog here. But a note about one benefit of short assignments is warranted: the greater likelihood of quicker feedback for the student. Recall that Csikszentmihalyi's definition of *flow states* includes the condition of ongoing, quick feedback (1990). Students who find larger assignments somewhat intimidating may flourish with shorter assignments, in part because of the feedback speed and frequency.

In my discussion in Chapter 9 of the need to balance repetition and variety, I noted that including common elements in every unit gives a degree of security to students, especially to those who require more tightly defined learning experiences. In science teaching, for example, students' knowledge that they will design and carry out an experiment every week or at some other frequency (Chapter 9: Repetition and Variety) gives them a sense of predictability and safety. It also builds connections between units and therefore coherence—harmony—in the course (Chapter 6).

The third implication of the principle that designs achieve harmony by incorporating a range of sizes is that the units in a course should be in a range of sizes. Rarely does a jurisdiction specify exactly how classroom teachers are to divide up the school year in their efforts to meet the specified learning outcomes for each unit in a particular subject and grade. Given that freedom, another suitable response to the need for variety of sizes is in varied unit lengths.

Jurisdictions may not admit as much when they publish standards, learning outcomes, or programs of studies, but in most courses some units function as centres (Chapter 3), like the columns that hold up the roof of a classical building, and other units do not. After teaching a course a couple times, most teachers understand which units are more important and begin to allocate more time to them. Less important units get less time. Some teachers tailor their overall (course) grading scheme to reflect the differing time allocated to the various units and others do not. Those who do not, even if they have not heard of Vitruvius or Alberti, might argue that a course in which every unit receives the same grade allocation has an undeniable symmetry.

## Hiding the Volume in Architecture

For a variety of reasons, some buildings need to be large. The cost of city-centre land compels architects and designers to build upwards. The sheer floor area needed for modern warehouses combines with the necessity for forklifts and roller-blading fulfilment pickers to navigate on level floors, yielding single-storey building designs covering hectares of land. Designers of these warehouses concern themselves with cost and efficiency more than with aesthetics, but designers of buildings in the city centre must meet a major aesthetic challenge: how to hide or camouflage large volumes to improve the aesthetic experience of those at street level. Most buildings are meant to invite, not to intimidate, and architects must find the meeting point between size and invitation.

**FIGURE 10.3** A telecom switching centre in Edmonton, Alberta

**FIGURE 10.4** Bodiam Castle, East Sussex, England

Some buildings are designed to repel and intimidate, not to invite. Telecom switching centres, for example (as in Figure 10.3) or castles (as in Figure 10.4) are designed specifically to keep people out. "Don't come in, don't even look in," seems to be the message sent architecturally by these unwelcoming structures.

Albert Speer, commonly known as Hitler's architect, designed but was never able to construct what the Third Reich envisioned as the largest dome ever built. The Great Hall, also known by the warmer but deceptive *Volkshalle* (Hall of the People), was to serve as a classical and monumental symbol of the final victory of Nazism. *Triumph of the Will*, Leni Riefenstahl's chilling story of Hitler's visit to the Nazi Party Rally in Nuremberg in 1934, gives one a deeper, graphic understanding of the sense of power that motivated Speer to design intimidating buildings.

In her children's book, *A Wrinkle in Time*, Madeleine L'Engle describes a building eerily similar to Speer's design. It is ". . . a strange, domelike building. Its walls glowed with a flicker of violet flame. Its silvery roof pulsed with ominous light." Once inside, "Meg could feel a rhythmical pulsing . . ." (1962, p. 156). With Nazism fading from memory and knowing what we now know about how social media networks vacuum up our personal information, we may now be more inclined to associate L'Engle's nightmare building with telecom switching buildings than with Albert Speer's imperial vision. I will return shortly to my (instructional design) purpose for giving even two paragraphs of this book over to buildings meant to intimidate with their volume. For now, let me end this brief treatment by noting that some clearly do not want to solve the problem of volume; they want the mass to show.

Architects have given much more effort to the project of hiding mass and volume. They have available only a limited number of approaches to this task. Designing the building to sit comfortably in its context—with a plaza out front for example—allows people to view the edifice from farther back and thereby helps reduce intimidation. Varying the cladding on a building helps. A building clad in nothing but glass emphasizes the building's height and does nothing to reduce the appearance of volume. Likewise, buildings in the international style, with their glass and stainless steel, tend to emphasize rather than reduce the appearance of height and volume.

Early in the history of skyscrapers, architects began using the *setback* as a means of reducing the appearance of mass and volume in tall buildings. Simply defined, the setback means that the entire tower of a sky-scraper cannot extend to the sidewalk, thereby reducing the appearance of height for anyone at street level. In one of the most common forms, what some call the *sidewalk wall* extends only four or five storeys from the ground. The architect builds in another setback after an additional five or six storeys, then designs the tower. In the first years of the 20th century, New York architects and the corporations who employed them began competing to build the tallest building in the world. Several factors, including the loss of light at street level, induced the city to make the setback into law in 1916. For those interested, contrasting accounts of the law and its effects are available in Abramson (2001) and van Leeuen's (1986) histories of the skyscraper (2001; 1986), as well as one article (Hoffmann, 1970). Also see the Wikipedia article, "1916 Zoning Resolution."

The reductions afforded by the setback are not only visual. Setbacks reduce the actual volume of the building in which they are used, as illustrated by The Canada Life Building in Toronto (Figure 10.1) and dozens of older buildings in New York, Chicago, and other cities. The New York resolution in 1916 deserves much of the credit for the increase in popularity enjoyed by the setback for two full decades. But it was later eclipsed by other styles. At the time of this writing, it is enjoying a revival, as illustrated by the 2017 Vogue condominium building in Calgary (Figure 10.5), a building that succeeds at making its entrance clear as well (Chapter 5). This revival comes partly because city dwellers increasingly desire surroundings on a human, rather than super-human, scale. Apart from the specific question of the skyscraper and the setback, hundreds of accessible treatments of the concept of scale in architecture are available (including Hoyt, 1981; Moore & Allen, 1976).

The French language contains a great, if somewhat archaic, phrase to catch the concern that buildings look good from the sidewalk. That is *étage de parade*. From the sidewalk or street, people viewing a building will inevitably cast their

**FIGURE 10.5** The Vogue, a 35-storey multi-use residential tower in Calgary, Alberta, illustrates both the setback and the obvious entrance

eyes on its first floor. In a sense, this will be the floor—the stage—that shows. With a skyscraper, our eyes may first go up. We want to take in the whole and we want to assess its height or perhaps its volume. But our eyes will finally come back to the ground floor, in part because we will look for its entrance and for its connection to the street. I intentionally used the word *shows* above to catch this sense of the word *parade* in French. The ground floor—the floor that shows—is on parade or display. In many places, historically, this floor will have been decorated more ornately than the floors above. It was designed to attract.

This idea of the *étage de parade* contains two important insights about the first day of a class. Obviously, and as I argued in Chapter 5 (Entrances and Exits), we should plan the first day of class so it invites and excites our students; this is the day when our students get their first view from the sidewalk, so to speak. But, to combine the concept of the setback with the concept of *étage de parade*, perhaps we should not reveal on the first day the size or volume of the unit, especially if students might be overwhelmed by finding out on their first day just how substantial that unit is.

**FIGURE 10.6** Apartments in Paris illustrate the concept of *étage de parade*

In this section I have dealt mainly with the setback and the French tradition of decorating the ground floor so it pleased the eye. Architects have other techniques for disguising height and volume. Window styles, cladding (surfaces), horizontal elements in tall buildings, and vertical elements in sprawling buildings are all pressed into service. Clear and inviting entrances such as that on the Vogue Condominium (Figure 10.5) reduce the intimidation and enhance the invitation. Elements outside the building such as plazas, playgrounds, sculptures, and landscaping contribute as well. I noted earlier in the chapter that literally hundreds of architects and designers have addressed the challenge of hiding the volume, and I will repeat no more of their accumulated wisdom here.

## Hiding the Volume in Instructional Design

Two complimentary approaches come to mind here, and I will argue them both briefly. First, we can introduce the complete scope of the contents in a given course, unit, or theme slowly by initially hiding some of the volume. Second, and obviously, we can break what is large into smaller parts. The course becomes units or themes, the units or themes become sub-themes or smaller topics, the sub-themes become days and lessons, the days and lessons become activities. In larger and more difficult units, we can combine these two approaches.

In the same way that architects take steps to improve the street view for those near large buildings, educators need to take steps to reduce the intimidation factor with new units. When students view a new unit, by definition, they view it from their perspective. Our challenge as their teachers may be to share some of our perspective on the volume and, more so, the character, of a unit. For example, we know about the experience of previous cohorts of students with this material. If previous cohorts have found the unit accessible we should say so. We should tell our students if previous cohorts have typically produced better work on this unit than on some other units, or if they have found it interesting and enjoyable. These suggestions may be especially important in the case of larger, intimidating units that contain more difficult concepts than other units in the course.

How do we disguise some of the volume in those units? Perhaps the word disguise connotes deception, in which case I ask how can we scaffold the introduction of the unit? I begin with the setback, the staged introduction, a good means of helping our students get a human-scale view of what lies ahead. The pedagogical concern that we not undermine student self-efficacy parallels the architectural concern that the street-view invite, not repel the viewer. Regardless of how substantive the unit actually is, we present it so that students think they can manage it.

In early January in the semester I wrote this chapter, I posted three documents on the course wiki for a three-credit course I have been teaching this semester. After what felt like endless editing, I managed to get the syllabus down to seven pages, including the requisite paragraphs about plagiarism, academic accommodations, university-wide grading definitions, departmental attendance policies, and so on. But I created that relatively succinct syllabus (by today's standards) only by producing *Readings*, a separate, five-page course bibliography, and by moving the detailed descriptions of the assignments into a separate document called *Rubrics* (which runs 20 pages). I confess to this overwork not to lament how syllabi have grown over the last several decades, but to underline the importance of not overwhelming or intimidating my students on the first day with the impression or misimpression that they have just begun the most difficult course ever offered anywhere. To use the metaphor of *étage de parade*, the first floor they see is decorated to invite. Those who read carefully will apprehend the volume in the course that lies ahead. But the first impression I want my students to get is that the course is manageable. In this case, I did not act deceptively, but separating the documents allowed me to keep the Assignments section of the syllabus brief. Asking what syllabi looked and felt like to students (the UX, the user-experience perspective) changed how I developed syllabi.

Elsewhere in this book, I have mentioned the three-column KWL sheet (What I **K**now, What I **W**ould like to know, What I **L**earned), which some teachers use as a private document (that only they and each respective student see) and some use to compile a whole-class wall display. Having students fill out the first two columns of a KWL sheet or one of its adaptations (Chapter 5: Entrances and Exits) helps students remember that they already know some things about the unit's contents. The KWL sheet moves both the teacher's design thinking and our discussion here to the matter of scaffolding. Using the KWL sheet to find out what the students know allows the teacher to reveal the unit in stages suited to the students' familiarity with the materials (and to add coherence, Chapter 6). Having argued in Chapter 5 for the grand entrance, I must flag the KWL sheet as, at best, a mid-voltage strategy. No one should view KWL as the main activity in the launch of a new unit. Still, it can serve an important focus with reference to scale.

My proposal that we introduce the volume in stages fits with Marzano's argument that learning proceeds more efficiently if students receive information in small segments (2007). In the same way that the course becomes units or themes, the units or themes become sub-themes or smaller topics, the sub-themes become days, and the days become activities. The small segments argument also fits with Csikszentmihalyi's work on *flow states*, which I mentioned earlier in the chapter. Introducing the work in bits allows us to give assessments with lower weights. Teachers who use the 5%, 10%, 20%, 40% formula for differentiating the weights of assignments in a unit usually design the unit with some low-weight assignments early. Early and regular feedback supports their students' sense of self-efficacy. Weaker students especially can get some work done and recorded in the first few days of a unit.

At the end of the previous section, I noted that architects and designers have developed many ways other than the setback and the decoration of the ground floor to render the street-view less intimidating for those passing by. I listed window styles, cladding, entrances and other elements. Without going into detail here, I will note that every principle I have dealt with in Chapters 3 to 9 can help increase students' self-efficacy in the cases of difficult and large, otherwise intimidating units. I have noted several times in this volume that these principles, together, form a language. That is important to remember when we consider the most challenging portions of our courses.

## Conclusion

Shifting perspectives, I close the chapter by comparing the design and presentation of a unit to that of a photo-copier. The size of the photo-copier does not intimidate its users, but its complexity does. Some of us even feel the apprehension grow as we physically approach it, wondering if it will select the correct paper, if it will jam, if the stapler is working, if it has a sensor that can tell we are in a hurry. Our questions may be parallel to the apprehensions some of our students feel as they approach new units.

But think about how the photo-copier keeps the most complicated parts out of sight and lets us see only the simplest parts: plastic covers and doors. The designers of copiers know about user experience (UX) and have located the control panel at the front where we can get at it. When things work as they should, we simply type in a code or run a card through a reader, drop our originals in the top bin, answer some questions, and then push "Copy." When we need to produce pdfs, we push "E-mail" and "Send" and a PDF magically goes to our email account. But how complex are the scanner and printer hidden behind the plastic covers and doors? Very. And we usually do not see or need to deal with these complex devices.

Those not persuaded by the comparison to the large building may find the copier a more useful metaphor. Taking a UX perspective raises some good questions about the ways we initially present the unit. Should teachers hide the more complex parts and inner workings underneath simple covers and doors? Can we initially present the unit by showing only the simplest and most accessible parts? Do students know how to get help when they encounter a jam? My answer to these questions is yes, we should.

## References

Abramson, D. M. (2001). *Skyscraper rivals: The AIG building and the architecture of Wall Street*. New York: Princeton Architectural Press.

Alberti, L. B. (1988). *On the art of building in ten books: 1404–1472* (J. Rykwert, N. Leach, & R. Tavernor, Trans.). Boston, MA: MIT Press.

Csikszentmihalyi, M. (1990). *Flow: The psychology of optimal experience*. New York: Harper and Row.

Hoffmann, D. (1970). The setback skyscraper city of 1891: An unknown essay by Louis H. Sullivan. *Journal of the Society of Architectural Historians*, 29(2), 181–187.

Hoyt, C. K. (1981). *Interior spaces designed by architects*. New York: McGraw Hill.

L'Engle, M. (1962). *A wrinkle in time*. New York: Farrar Straus Giroux.

Marzano, R. J. (2007). *The art and science of teaching: A comprehensive framework for effective instruction*. Alexandria, VA: ASCD.

Moore, C., & Allen, G. (1976). *Dimensions: Space, shape and scale in architecture*. New York: McGraw Hill.

Pollio, V. (1960). *The ten books of architecture* (M. H. Morgan, Trans.). New York: Dover.

van Leeuwen, T. (1986). *The skyward trend of thought: The metaphysics of the American skyscraper*. Cambridge, MA: MIT Press.

**FIGURE 11.1** A street in Europe full of human life

# 11

# MASTER PLANS AND ORGANIC DEVELOPMENT

The street shown in Figure 11.1 has the potential to send some people to a travel web site and type in words such as "Provence" and "La Spezia." Why? What draws us? Many respond at a subconscious level to the warmth and simple humanity of such a scene. People are sitting, walking, eating, relaxing, shopping. But there is more on this street. The street itself has been repaired, over centuries. Some paving stones do not match the rest. The mix of buildings points to the absence of a master-plan, although successive planning departments must have worked consistently to preserve the character and tone they desired. To be somewhat crude, this street was not assembled from what the British call a flat-pack. Rather it evolved over time. Generations of workers contributed to its physical construction and maintenance. And generations of coffee-drinkers, parents with children, strolling tourists, and shoe-buyers gave it its character.

In other words, it developed organically, not by master-planning. This chapter compares the development of the squares, villages and streets where people feel most deeply alive to the development of great courses, units, and lessons. At its simplest, I will argue that they develop the same way, not by master-planning, but by long human occupation and regular repair.

## A Teaching Challenge in its Context

Nearly every experienced educator—whether in elementary, secondary or higher education—has endured an educational master-planning nightmare. In higher education, these nightmares take such forms as curriculum revisions, changes from a 3-credit system to 4, moves from face-to-face to online instruction, and the creation of new programs or colleges. Elementary and secondary teachers regularly hear that their department of education or school district has adopted yet another new plan for curriculum, instruction, or assessment and that they mean for teachers to implement it beginning at the start of the next school year. For a variety for reasons, many educators at all levels roll their eyes about master-planning. Some educators—presumably not those reading this paragraph—have lost their spark for teaching altogether, in part because of the succession of failed or withdrawn plans they have been mandated to implement during their careers. But even among those where the spark still glows, one finds cynicism rooted in the memory of how many previous programs, initiatives, mission-statement revisions, and curriculum master-plans arrived with similar hype, only to be forgotten or jettisoned within two or three years in favor of new and supposedly better ideas.

Even if they do not articulate it quite this way, perhaps a few seasoned educators have an intuitive sense that educational master plans often flounder for the simple reason that central planners cannot predict teachers' and students' responses to new initiatives. New circumstances arise. Local contexts influence reception. Humans notoriously do not behave predictably. There are simply too many kinds of students and too many unique classroom circumstances for any central office or department of education to produce one plan that will fit all. A centrally-generated master plan might envision teachers and students doing this, over here, but some usually end up doing that, over there.

Individual teachers often experience the same with our own instructional plans, not just our year or semester plans but even with our plans for a week's instruction or a lesson or two. We make our plans, envisioning that we will give very clear and specific instructions and then our students, who will understand those clear instructions, will busy themselves working and learning. But, in the classroom moment, we discover that we omitted something from the instructions, that what we included lacked the clarity we were certain it possessed, that we forgot to bring some of the needed materials, or that one student was allergic to latex. We abandon our plans. Or we muddle through, perhaps with some students who do understand assisting those who do not. Though not at the scale of a failed jurisdiction-wide initiative, our own in-class plans sometimes suffer a similar fate.

An example of planning gone awry comes from my own university classroom, where I tried a new learning/teaching strategy—speed-dating—for the first time while working on this chapter. Twenty-nine students and I were to pitch the strengths and note the weaknesses of 30 different orientations to curriculum and philosophies of education to each other. In my plan, each person had 90 seconds to present to his or her conversation partner, so each pair would spend just over three minutes in their exchange. When the appointed time-keeper would call time, half the people would move one seat to the right (on what we started calling the *conveyor belt*) and half would sit still. With a bit of quick math, you can figure out that with this system in place, in about 50 minutes—what I called round one—any given student would have exchanged ideas with half the class.

We would need a second round to allow those who had sat still in round one to talk to the others who had sat still in round one, and those who had moved in round one to talk to the others who had moved in round one. I planned my solution to that problem by planning a round two (and also rounds three and four). Search *teaching strategy speed dating* online, work through the instructions on some of the sites that appear, and you will see how complex it actually can be. I have provided plenty of detail about how speed-dating was supposed to work so will be brief about how it did work: there was confusion and chaos, most of it due to my own poor explanation at the beginning of the activity. I will come back to speed-dating later in the chapter. My point here is that the best laid plans did not work as they were supposed to do.

While implementation misadventures are no reason to abandon planning, they do point to the need to think about planning differently from how many of us typically think about it. To refer to a key concept in the design work of Kees Dorst (2015) we need to reframe how we think about planning curriculum and instruction. We need to reframe because people respond to grand curriculum plans, and even modest curriculum plans, even day-to-day teaching plans, unpredictably. So, I propose that we reframe our thinking about planning by identifying some of the qualities of places where master-planning failed to produce good results compared to the villages, towns, cities, and buildings where humans feel most comfortable and where they feel grateful simply to be alive. How did these places that are so easy to love come to be great? What role did planning play in producing them? And what role did long human occupation play? And how do design and planning connect to each other in our own thinking about the units that we wish were great?

## A Parallel Problem in Design

Designers, town planners, architects, artists, and even writers face similar problems to those we face as educators. A design or plan begins as a grand design or a grand plan. But gaps appear between the plan and the unfolding work. In fact, an academic field called *implementation science* has emerged in the last few decades, focusing on how and why the results of new research are or are not implemented in such fields as medicine, public policy, and education. The phrase and the field may both be relatively new, but human interest in the gaps between what is known or planned and what eventually happens is as old as the ancient saying, *there's many a slip between cup and lip.*

For about one minute, think about a Stalinesque Moscow apartment complex. Then think about the streets, plazas, courtyards, and buildings in European towns and villages that people find pleasing or life-giving. What generates the contrast between these images? What qualities characterize the Soviet apartment block? Without either nuance or prejudice, I suggest that the Soviet apartment block was meant to house a lot of people rationally, efficiently and

**FIGURE 11.2** An apartment block that appears to have no soul

economically (to use the language of Duany, Plater-Zyberk, and Speck, 2000). And it was built to a master plan; that is, a central authority determined what regions of the country required housing and then planned that housing in specific areas of specific cities in those regions. If my assumption that the goal of the plan was to house many people efficiently and economically then the program was a qualified success. Implementation science specialists would have to admit that the plans in question were realized. However, today these housing blocks are considered paradigms of ugliness and symbols of modern arrogance and the failures of central planning.

A long tradition of architects, designers, and writers agree that the problem with master-planned projects is that in their very design they ignore the actual patterns of people's lives, both inside and outside their homes (for example, see Allsopp, 1974). In an essay in the edited collection, *Gehry Draws,* architect Frank Gehry addresses this question of paying attention to the patterns of people's lives. He states, "When I start a project, I inform myself a lot about the project requirements and the people involved. And then I work in the models—trying things, trying forms, looking. I try something and I take it off, then I try it again, and the whole work slowly evolves, a piece at a time. If I too consciously premeditate, I don't enjoy it. I don't find it as exciting, and the end result isn't as good. Sometimes when I'm presenting a project I don't know where I'm going beyond a certain point" (Gehry, Rappolt, & Violette, 2005, p. 256).

Others echo Gehry's comments about this iterative, uncertain approach to design. In fact, designers and architects approach designs tentatively in part

**FIGURE 11.3** A master–planned neighbourhood

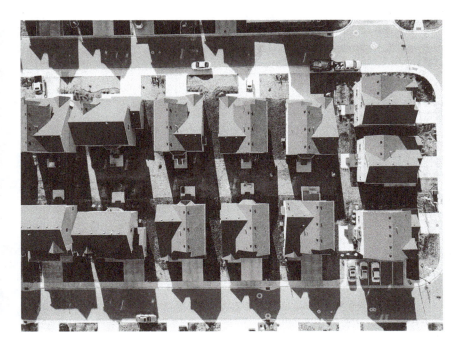

**FIGURE 11.4** Boxes that mostly look just the same

because they cannot possibly know in advance how things will look or how people will respond; there are simply too many variables (Lawson, 2004). Chapter 12 includes a short section on the messiness and iterative character of the design process that connects to the shortcomings of master planning. The essence of that section is that much design knowledge can be learned only through practice. Stewart Brand, famous for founding and editing the *Whole Earth Catalogue*, wrote in this vein. Adapting the open building philosophy of Dutch architect John Habraken, he argues in *How Buildings Learn* (1994) that builders should wait a couple years to see where people walk before building the sidewalks in a development. He meant this literally but also as a more metaphorical constraint on master planning; we need to wait and see. Brand's clever title actually reverses the real gist of his argument; he wants the people who use buildings to learn.

Several master planned cities illustrate the verity of these claims about the limitations of master planning and the need to wait and see. Balmopan was master-planned as a new capital city of Belize after Hurricane Hattie destroyed much of Belize City in 1961. One assumes that a hurricane leaves a city with more than its share of roughness (to use a term Ruskin loved). Yet, most in the Belize story preferred a destroyed city that they thought of as their own to the new, master-planned city conceived in a central office. Brasilia also comes to mind. With examples of relatively successful master-planning such as Paris and Philadelphia in mind, the Brazilian government created a city that fell far short of the Paris in the rain forest originally planned.

Balmopan and Brasilia notwithstanding, all is not lost. Architects and town planners have suggested approaches and adaptations with great potential to achieve the opposite of what I have described in the above paragraphs.

## Solutions to the Design Problem

My interest in this part of the chapter is in how haphazard plans, non-plans, and imperfect plans can help lead to great results. In the non-curricular world, the best buildings, towns and cities do not usually result from master plans; they evolve piecemeal and organically by long habitation and use, reflecting the patterns of life that people actually choose as they dwell in, use, and adapt those buildings, towns and cities. These places show *ad hoc* development, maintenance and repair, and their *patina* reveals the long-term wear and tear of human occupation and use. (This theme runs thorugh all Alexander's work and also appears in Wharton, 1897, p. 117)

Provence, occupied by Greeks, Celts, Romans, Moors, and Italians, known for being built up over time in a variety of styles, openly shows many signs of change, wear and tear, damage and repair (Jacobs, 1994). In recent decades, Provence has gained a reputation as a special place where one may go to find peace, quiet, or even love, thanks in part to books such as Peter Mayle's *A Year in Provence* (1990) or *The Most Beautiful Villages of Provence* by Michael Jacobs

(1994). (No doubt, these titles have done more to feed Provence's image as a magical place than did Julius Caesar's multi-volume *Gallic Wars*.) But behind the mythology are some specific attracting qualities, one of which is that the centuries of human occupation—the wear and tear—show everywhere and so clearly, and they bespeak a kind of warmth. The patina betrays life. The Provence that locals and visitors love today is not the result of a master plan. Rather it is what it is because generations of people have lived there and adapted and repaired it to suit their own circumstances and needs.

The villages of Provence show patina and roughness that, by definition, one cannot find in Seaside, the picture-perfect town in Florida designed by Andres Duany and Elizabeth Plater-Zyber where Peter Weir filmed *The Truman Show*. Nor will one find much patina or roughness in Celebration, Florida, the new-urbanist town the Disney corporation created from scratch near Orlando. In old towns and villages, texture and imperfections convey uniqueness and life. In neither architecture nor education can anyone simply build in from the start the kind of character most of us love in old buildings, towns, and cities.

Christopher Alexander argues at many points for letting imperfection and the wear and tear of long occupation show. Three works especially warrant mention in this context. The first is a short chapter with the intriguing, irresistible title, "The Perfection of Imperfection" (1991). Those who build will find this most

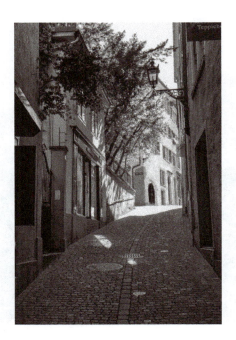

**FIGURE 11.5** A street with evidence of long habitation and use

interesting, but all educators will take courage from his argument that the places humans feel most at home are rarely perfect. To the extent that classrooms and curriculum are where we and our students live for big parts of our days, Alexander's chapter will come as encouragement. In "A City is not a Tree," originally published in two parts in 1965 and 1966, Alexander pursued some of the same questions about imperfection and its relationship to how cities become great (2015). *The Oregon Experiment* (1975) tells the story of Alexander and his colleagues' work over several years with the University of Oregon. Although it is a thin volume, it makes a compelling argument for organic growth attuned to the actual ways people use buildings and the spaces between them. And the title warrants our attention as educators; in Alexander's view, the University of Oregon campus was an experiment, not the result of single, grand vision.

I end this section by referring again to the work of John Ruskin. He used the phrase "fantastic paradox" to describe his view that ". . . no architecture can be truly noble, which is not imperfect" (2005, p. 25). A page later he argued that ". . . the demand for perfection is always a sign of a misunderstanding of the ends of art." Another page later, he asserts that ". . . imperfection is in some sort essential to all that we know of life. It is the sign of life in a mortal body, that is to say, of a state of progress and change" (p. 27). Just prior to the pages from which I drew these quotations, Ruskin compared imperfect hand-made Venetian

**FIGURE 11.6** A quiet lane that speaks of warmth and comfort

glass to flawless manufactured glass. On his account, no two pieces of Venetian glass are the same, and the imperfections of Venetian glass come with the variety (Chapter 9 in this book). To anticipate the next section in my chapter, the teacher wanting to employ a variety of teaching-learning strategies will need to attempt new approaches and will inevitably make mistakes. In class as in glass, with variety will come with imperfection.

## Solutions in Curriculum and Instruction

As I have noted repeatedly in previous chapters, the approaches designers and architects have taken to their challenges have great potential to help us with ours. In this case, if we apply some of their insights, we can reduce some of our frustrations with designs and plans that unfold in unanticipated ways. I believe this to be true both with new master plans that originate outside our classrooms and with our own instructional plans.

Veteran educators know the same truth about great courses; obviously a school, program or course must be planned—and architects and town planners concede this about buildings, towns and cities—but a great school, program, or course results organically, through long human occupation. It evolves as a school, department, or teacher and successive cohorts of students work through it, tinkering, making adjustments, adding and subtracting parts, adapting and changing as they go. Like the great building or town, the great curriculum, course, unit, or even lesson also evolves in an organic, ad hoc, piecemeal way; it usually does not result from design and planning alone. In the remainder of this section I suggest four specific ideas for curriculum and instruction we can adopt from the practice of architects, town planners, and designers.

The first practice to extract from the work of architects and designers is to make small or even large revisions to our plans in light of students' responses to them. We drop an assignment because it did not work. We plan more time for this or that section. We substitute this material for that other material because it meets our objectives equally well but involves a writer or topic the students find more interesting at this time. Given that we do this constant revision, allow me the simple suggestion that we tell our students, "A couple years ago a student asked for X so here it is," or "Last semester, students asked me to take assignment X out of the course, but if any of you find this topic interesting, I would be happy to substitute it for this other assignment. Just talk to me after class." Sometimes we make those changes because of our own boredom, especially in those signature courses of which we annually teach multiple sections. Sometimes we implement changes as a means of keeping our brain alive, a matter I take up again in Chapter 12.

To illustrate my suggestion about revisions, I return to my earlier description of my foray into instructional speed-dating. The chaos and how we addressed it are key to the idea of organic development. The deficiencies of the plan evidenced themselves early; what I had planned was clearly imperfect. But we fixed it on the fly and kept going. To compare that class to a building or a street, by the time we finished the lesson it showed some signs of wear and tear. It showed evidence of human habitation. The morning after that lesson, on the course web site, I posted an invitation for anyone from the class to improve the instructions. After all, middle-schoolers could do speed dating with the names and main characteristics of mammals, plants, jurisdictions and capitals, regions and main products, nations and main languages. Secondary-schoolers could speed-date with the elements and the main compounds and where we find each of them in common household products, or they could speed date with political leaders and their published agendas. Two students took up my invitation, and the next time I use this method, I will name them as the ones who improved the instructions. The strategy will bespeak human life, both because a class of my living students endured its trial run and because two students took up the challenge to improve it.

Something quite important happened in class a week after our speed-dating adventure. After I lamented about the glitches in executing the speed-dating strategy (perhaps I used the word flop), one student reminded me that one of the course readings was a chapter called "Juicy Mistakes," from William Westney's book on piano pedagogy, *The Perfect Wrong Note* (2003, pp. 51–76). I had asked my students to read Westney's material because he outlines what I call a philosophy of mistakes, something my pre-service teachers need as they work with students and as they work through their own flops in classrooms. The student reminding me of Westney wanted me not to beat myself over what went wrong on my first attempt to use speed-dating in class. I could learn from what happened and move on, exactly as Westney suggested. She spared me by not pointing out the additional irony that in our course textbook, *The Courage to Teach*, Parker Palmer discussed our flops and our fears (1998, pp. 35–60). In teaching, as in towns and cities, we will not reach perfection, but we can fix and change as we go. If teaching is indeed a craft, as Alan argued in his 1984 book, then we should all be ready to work at our craft and to learn by doing.

A second strategy we can extract from those who have written about the organic growth of great places is to accept that imperfection comes with the pedagogical territory. Perfect teachers likely need to build imperfection in intentionally. For most of us, roughness and imperfection show up uninvited. Nevertheless, we can make room for and perhaps build in a little roughness here and there. In an age when some syllabi are approaching twenty pages and when students demand a detailed grading rubric for every assignment, let me repeat the suggestion from Chapter 10 that we initially withhold a few details when we present the course to our students. Some educators even present the syllabus with grade ranges specified instead of exact grade allocations, inviting students for their views on what weights should be given to various assignments. Presenting what looks to some like an unfinished syllabus might cause some discomfort, and co-determining the grading schema requires some negotiating, but it does increase student engagement. One need not give a lot of instructional time over to such a task. In junior or senior high, students could meet in groups for as few as ten minutes and then submit their proposals in writing. The same approach works with date ranges instead of specific dates for assignments.

A third strategy comes from the passage from Frank Gehry I quoted earlier. He admitted in writing and seemed to say he admits to clients that he sometimes does not "know where [he is] going beyond a certain point" (p. 256). I am aware that educators do not all agree about whether or not we should admit that we do not know something. I believe that we can—we should—tell students that when we do not know the answer to their question we should say so. The imperfect handout or on-screen presentation fits this category as well. Many teachers spend too much time perfecting their materials. We need to remember that imperfection and roughness speak to our humanity.

## Conclusion

Educators have written many books and articles on how to construct or teach a great course. Were Christopher Alexander to write such a book, I believe he would say that you cannot design a great course in detail from the ground up. Rather, you plan it and then year after year, as successive cohorts of students work through it with you, you fix, heal, subtract and add to that course as you go. We come back to where we started: we know a course must be planned, but a great course can only be assembled by a teacher and several cohorts of students.

## References

Alexander, C. (1991). The perfection of imperfection. In H. Junker (Ed.), *Roots and branches: Contemporary essays by west coast writers* (pp. 204–214). San Francisco, CA: Mercury House.
Alexander, C., & Mehaffy, M. (2015). *A city is not a tree*. Portland, OR: Sustasis Press.
Alexander, C., Silverstein, M., Angel, S., Ishikawa, S., & Abrams, D. (1975). *The Oregon experiment*. New York: Oxford University Press.
Allsopp, B. (1974). *Towards a humane architecture*. Edinburgh, UK: Frederick Muller.
Brand, S. (1994). *How buildings learn: What happens after they're built*. New York: Viking.
Dorst, K. (2015). *Frame innovation: Create new thinking by design*. Cambridge, MA: MIT Press.
Duany, A., Plater-Zyberk, E., & Speck, J. (2000). *Suburban nation: The rise of sprawl and the decline of the American dream*. New York: North Point Press.
Gehry, F., Rappolt, M., & Violette, R. (2005). *Gehry draws*. London: Violette.
Jacobs, M. (1994). *The most beautiful villages of Provence*. New York: Thames and Hudson.
Lawson, B. (2004). *What designers know*. Amsterdam: Architectural Press.
Mayle, P. (1990). *A year in Provence*. New York: Knopf/Vintage.
Palmer, P. (1998). *The courage to teach*. San Francisco, CA: Jossey-Bass.

Ruskin, J. (2005). *The nature of gothic.* New York: Penguin Books.

Tom, A. R. (1984). *Teaching as a moral craft.* New York: Longman.

Westney, W. (2003). *The perfect wrong note.* Pompton Plains, NJ: Amadeus Press.

Wharton, E. (1897). *The decoration of houses.* New York: Norton.

**FIGURE 11.7** Momentarily empty of human life, a corner still speaks of life

**FIGURE 12.1** Erasmus Bridge in Rotterdam, The Netherlands by Ben van Berkel

**FIGURE 12.2** Concrete box girders combine with arches to connect the islands of Skye and Eilean Bàn near Lochalsh, north-western Scotland

# 12

# AGILE, LIGHT STRUCTURES

The metaphor I build in this chapter draws parallels between the forces that educators and students face and the forces that engineers and architects must take into account when they design roofs and bridges. As one clever student put it, gravity sucks, and anyone wanting to design a structure that will stand up to gravity will need to work with the principles of mathematics and physics (and possibly chemistry) to prevent that structure from falling down. In the beginning of the chapter, I catalogue some of the pressures students and teachers experience. The second and third parts of the chapter focus on the forces that act on bridges and roofs. In these sections, I review how the designers of such structures transfer those forces to the ground. I close the chapter by arguing that educators can find ways—parallel to those developed by the designers of physical structures—to transfer classroom forces to the educational ground.

## The Stressors and Pressures in Classrooms

Students face a variety of forces and stresses from both inside and outside of school. Forces originating inside school buildings obviously include their academic progress, but also their success in sports, music, drama, and other clubs, as well as how they are getting along with their school friends. Hans Selyé, the McGill University endocrinologist who originally imported the word stress from the field of metallurgy to medicine and psychology, concluded that even life's good things act as stressors on our systems (1956, 1974). On his account, being passed over for a school team and being picked for a school team both act as stressors on the student.

Outside their schools, students read the same world and local news their teachers read, both good and bad. They celebrate the same victories and lament the same disasters. In relation to family, friends, and relationships, they experience the same joys and sorrows from the same kinds of sources as do their teachers. Again, according to Selyé, joys and sorrows both exert forces on a person.

We know that some pressures on students may be more perceived than real. Students may feel overworked because they have overestimated how much time some of their assignments will require. Individual students and whole classes can underestimate their grasp of the learning materials. And, as every teacher knows, some stress is self-induced because students procrastinate. On the other hand, some student anxiety may be well-founded, especially about grades and assessment. A student may feel real pressure because he or she has not done well in a given term. Students in some classes and schools (and nations) have too much work. Some may feel real pressure because they have a surplus of other commitments in their lives. Finally, because they have been in school from an early age, many students have developed a distorted understanding of the purposes of education. For good reasons, they may have come to believe that only what can be counted counts. Having inhaled the culture of assessment as a natural part of the air they breathe for a significant part of their lives, they have lost the capacity for wonder and the inherent desire to learn with which they may have started school many years before they came to our class.

Educators must handle many of the same forces and pressures as their students, but they also experience some forces of which most students remain unaware. These can be classified initially into the familiar categories of curriculum, instruction, and assessment. They include, first of all, the concern that one's students meet the jurisdiction's learning outcomes. Teachers also need to respond to mandates to incorporate new curriculum initiatives from their school or jurisdiction. Obviously, instructional pressures include managing instructional materials. Teachers need to have their materials ready for each class and they need to put those materials away after use. They need to design and plan new units in several courses or classes. They must carry out day-to-day preparation for instruction, while making adaptations and accommodations for exceptional students.

Assessment brings other challenges. For many teachers, the constant challenge of getting grading done and handed back to students within a reasonable time is a major source of stress (and guilt). Teachers care that all their students succeed, and they worry more about the weakest ones. Of course, the desire for our students' success arises out of altruistic motives, but we know that their successes— or, more pointedly, their possible failures—ultimately reflect on our professional abilities as well, so assessment functions as another kind of force, one linked to but less altruistic than wanting what is best for our students.

We do the work of curriculum, instruction, and assessment in one kind of classroom ethos or another, and that ethos (which the educational databases generally call *climate*) is largely built by us. And building that ethos takes work. The educator who lists respect, curiosity, or joy among her classroom ideals knows that once class starts—and between classes—she does not get a moment off. It takes constant attention to realize ideals, including attention to administrative tasks, which adds another set of forces to the teacher's week. Teachers serve on committees, work with budgets, learn new software systems, and communicate with students' parents and guardians. They keep records for all students, including more detailed records for students on individual education plans.

The five categories of curriculum, instruction, assessment, classroom climate, and administration are helpful to our analysis, and when we combine them we end up with a category that probably should be called *sheer workload*. Many teachers view the daily challenge of carving out time for lunch or finding time to go to the washroom as lenses through which to view the massive workload entailed in the teaching vocation. Using those two simple, daily challenges as a lens, some teachers see not only workload but actual problems with the structure of their vocation. This workload may simply be the combination of the five built-in aspects of teaching I listed (that lead to regular breaches of the labor code), but workload produces tiredness, then leads to weariness, and finally induces questioning about vocation and, for some, departure from the profession.

These forces must be transferred to the ground.

## A Parallel Problem in Design

The metaphor in this chapter began its life at summer camp in Saskatchewan. When I was a child, at every summer camp I attended I wondered why the builders of the dining hall had installed several steel cables or rods across the top of the side walls, always at about four-meter intervals and always with some kind of adjustable turnbuckle in the middle. A few years later, in my high-school construction class, I got my answer: the builders had to keep the roof's weight from pushing the walls out and thereby collapsing on the campers' heads. On a tight budget, cables or rods were the cheapest solution, albeit far from the most beautiful one. (Designers of airport terminals now put these rods on prominent display.) All buildings with a gable roof need to address these outward forces. In most homes, the ceiling rafters reach from one side of the house to the other, acting as *collar ties*, restraining the side walls from being pushed outward by the roof. Homes with cathedral ceilings use manufactured scissor trusses. These angled trusses give the appearance that the collar tie is absent and that the ceiling is attached to the roof when, in fact, the ceiling and roof are at two different angles and the collar tie is hidden from view just above the ceiling.

All designers and builders of roofs—including flat roofs—need to take into account the weight of the roof and anything that may be on it, including snow, water, helicopters, or even tourists. Designers and builders of angled roofs ordinarily do not worry about helicopters, tourists, or pools of rainwater, but, as I noted, they need to take account of the outward forces on the walls, which

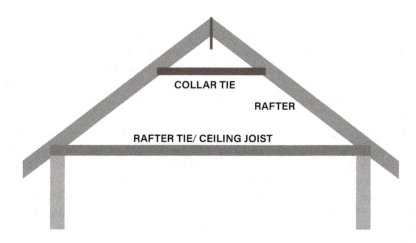

**FIGURE 12.3**  The lowest horizontal member of this roof structure functions as a collar tie to prevent the weight of the roof from pushing the walls outward

**FIGURE 12.4**  The top elements of the scissor truss support the roof. The bottom elements act as a collar tie to hold the side walls in place. They combine with the top elements and smaller pieces to transfer the forces outward and downward

must be transferred to the ground and prevented from pushing the walls out. Anyone interested in reading further about why the roofs above their heads stay where they do may find these two accessible volumes of interest: *Why Buildings Stand Up* and *Why Buildings Fall Down* (Levy & Salvadori, 1992; Salvadori, 1980).

The same forces work on bridges, and the same principles apply in bridge design. Bridges must handle the *dead load* (the weight of the bridge itself), the *live load* (the weight of traffic and snow), and the forces exerted on the structure by the wind. The dead load and live load are downward forces, and even though the bridge, roughly speaking, is a horizontal structure, these loads must somehow be transmitted to the ground. To withstand the force of wind, the bridge requires lateral strength so that it does not begin to sway and then collapse. Just as designers and builders of buildings must take into account the outward pressure on the walls caused by the downward pressure of the roof, bridge designers must find ways to transmit the dead and live weight of the bridge to its two ends, or to the ends plus one or more piers. Bridge designers would likely want to refine and nuance my description of the forces that act on bridges—given that I am an educator, not an engineer—but most of them would agree that I have identified the main structural issues.

Of course, one can span a short distance without difficulty, as illustrated by the bridge in Figure 12.5, built by friends of mine in the Gulf Islands of British Columbia. I built the arches for this bridge because my friends wanted the aesthetic quality of an arched deck as opposed to a flat deck, even though straight wooden floor joists would have sufficed structurally to support this relatively short span over what becomes a stream in the rainy season. In fact, I cut the arches out of straight fir floor joists and covered them in cedar, so in that sense, they are faux arches, not real ones.

Using a different principle to address the same problem of transferring forces to the ground, the people of Bhutan and Tibet built the first suspension bridges in the 1400s. These bridges were anchored directly to mountainsides, without towers. Thornton Wilder begins his moral fable, the *Bridge of San Luis Rey*, with a description of just such a simple suspension bridge, a structure familiar to all of us:

> On Friday noon, July the twentieth, 1714, the finest bridge in all Peru broke and precipitated five travelers into the gulf below. This bridge was on the high road between Lima and Cuzco and hundreds of persons passed

**FIGURE 12.5** Arched bridge where the main arches transfer the loads to the ground on either side. Smith residence, Gulf Islands, British Columbia

over it every day. It had been woven of osier by the Incas more than a
century before and visitors to the city were always led out to see it. It was
a mere ladder of thin slats swung out over the gorge, with handrails of
dried vine. . . . The bridge seemed to be among the things that last forever;
it was unthinkable that it should break.

(Wilder, 2004, p. 1)

Wilder set his story in 1714, and although we are more likely today to use
osier (grape) vines to make rattan furniture than to build bridges, the principles
governing bridge design remain the same. The suspension bridge as we know it
now, with its towers and steel cables, did not appear until the 1800s, but it
operates according to the same laws as the vine bridges in the Himalayas and in
Wilder's story, for these are the laws of physics.

Architects have imported the suspension principle to building design as well.
For example, the roof of the Scotiabank Saddledome hockey arena in my city,
Calgary, keeps its roof from falling on the players and spectators by means of
cables suspended from towers. In effect, it is several crisscrossed suspension
bridges, although mathematicians might refer to them as reverse hyperbolic
paraboloids. Given sufficient time and enough vines, the Incas could have built
the suspended roof on Calgary's Saddledome.

In short, bridges range from the faux arches on my friends' property in British
Columbia, to the first arches in Mesopotamia, to the simple vine or rope
suspension bridges built by locals in some mountainous regions, to Robert
Maillart's famous Salginatobel Bridge in Switzerland (in Figure 12.7, also see
Billington, 1979). Maillart's bridge relates to my metaphor in an important

**FIGURE 12.6** Nepalese suspension bridge built in the traditional style with modern
materials

**FIGURE 12.7** Robert Maillart's reinforced concrete Salginatobel Bridge (1930) near Shiers, in Canton Graubünden, eastern Switzerland

respect: it looks relaxed and at ease, it is not tense. It also looks like it fits in its context. Its elegance, in fact, is the source of the word *elegant* in the title of this book. All bridges, of whatever design, have important structural purposes in common: they all address the same challenge of transferring the weight of the bridge itself and its live load to the ground, and they all must withstand wind.

## Solutions to the Design Problem

Returning to roofs for a moment, medieval architects solved the problem of the outward forces placed on walls by heavy roofs with the flying buttress, especially in cathedrals (Figure 12.8). Flying buttresses, whether inside or outside the building, effectively transfer the roof's downward and outward forces to the ground. Some designers used a combination of flying buttresses and timber frame collar ties. That so many cathedrals remain upright in our own time speaks to the efficacy of this approach. The spaces created under flying buttresses were called vaults and the interior vaults were viewed as useable space (Acland, 1972; Fitchen, 1981; Gimpel, 1993; Stoddard, 1966).

Historically, bridge designers and builders have approached the gravity challenge several ways, the simplest of which I already noted. Some solutions use less material than others, some are capable of spanning greater distances than others, and some are more elegant than others. Figure 12.5 shows a bridge only three meters long. If I had attempted to build it out of toothpicks and marshmallows, as some primary students are called upon to do, or plastic drinking straws, as participants in team-building seminars are sometimes asked to do, the weakness of the materials would have forced me to take the laws of physics far more seriously. In this case, I could ignore those principles because I used hefty floor joists relative to the short span. Longer spans present the designer with a physics problem that the thickest laminated wood beams or even steel beams available today ultimately cannot solve (because as beam thickness increases, the dead load increases, ultimately negating the gains of thicker beams). This speaks to the question of the historical evolution of bridges. The Babylonians, lacking both laminated timbers and steel beams, addressed this longer-span problem by inventing the arch. The Romans were able to strengthen the arch and thereby lengthen its span when they invented cement.

Today, as part of our daily routine, many of us drive on an interstate highway or use a concrete bridge built sometime in the 1950s or 1960s, decades that, in retrospect, look less like the golden age of concrete and more like a nightmare of urban blight. Why so? Because road builders and bridge designers at the time usually overcame problems of physics not by using arches but by using concrete box girders to transfer the necessary loads. Box girders use the same technique as the engineered truss to transfer the downward forces outward to the ground or to the nearest piers. By that measure, they are effective. But, viewed from a distance, they look like solid concrete, not like hollow boxes, and, with some exceptions (such as the bridge in Figure 12.2) they lack the kind of elegance and beauty Robert Maillart achieved in the 1930s with his arched Salginatobel Bridge (Figure 12.7) or the aesthetic simplicity (but engineering complexity) of Santiago Calatrava's bridges today *or* Ben van Berkel's Erasmus bridge in Rotterdam

**FIGURE 12.8**  Flying buttresses relieve the walls of some of the outward forces placed on them by the roof. In this case, the buttresses are concealed inside another building

**FIGURE 12.9** Santiago Calatrava's Margaret Hunt Hull Bridge, in Dallas, Texas

(Figure 7.1). Road- and bridge-planners in the 1950s and 1960s, for the most part, solved construction challenges simply by pouring more cement. In other words, they frequently chose to forego what I have, in this volume, called design (and elegance) and they jumped straight into planning and building. My claims about the use of cement are not hyperbolic but are borne out by histories of the US interstate highway system, some of them naïve and even iconographic (for example, Swift, 2012) and others more critical (Lewis, 2013).

## Solutions in Classrooms and Teachers' Professional Lives

I started this chapter by surveying some of the demands of teaching that we might call *forces*, and now I want to explore how we might transfer those forces effectively. Having set up this structural loads metaphor, we come to the question that functions as the hinge in the chapter: do we transfer classroom forces to the educational ground by working with the laws that seem to govern human behavior naturally, or do we respond by trying to match force with force? Designers of roofs and bridges devised ways to transfer the relevant forces to the (physical) ground. Educators can also devise ways to handle the forces that act on students and teachers; we can transfer those forces to the educational ground. Indeed, we must. I begin this section by noting several inadequate responses to classroom forces, then explore several wise and workable approaches, some of them simple and even elegant.

### *Inadequate responses to classroom forces*

Classroom forces vary. The teacher or the students or a minority of students can come to class tired on a given day. This is the kind of force that affects how the classroom functions. A teacher could just have received good news about the health of a child or of a parent. The school's team could have just won an important game of basketball the night before, producing students who are excited that for the first time in years their school will be represented in the playoffs. This is a force that comes into the room. Good news or bad news, nationally, internationally, or even locally can affect students and teachers alike. Recalling the work on stress by Selyé again, both good news and bad generate forces that act on the structures in place in the room.

Some educators respond to classroom forces with the metaphorical equivalent of bolstering material strength, of adding to the thickness of the beam or the volume of the cement. Especially when the force in question is student resistance, some teachers try to overcome the force by loading on more work. Their motive may be to demonstrate to students the seriousness of staying focused. But, increasing the volume of work rarely solves the problem, and it might even intensify it because some students will add resentment to the resistance already present. A second response, quite similar to that one, is to adopt an authoritarian posture, which I have explored in print elsewhere (2017). Expressed as a sentence, this one runs, "Once they figure out who's boss in this room, they will do their work." The teacher adopting this mode may, in fact, get more of what sociologists call compliance; as the bulldozer can push aside a pile of dirt regardless of the dirt's wishes, the authoritarian teacher can overcome classroom forces. However, authoritarian classroom leadership can also generate the same kind of resistance that piling on more work generates. Instead of transferring real classroom forces to the ground, these approaches may add to the load the structure is required to carry, like shoveling more snow onto one's roof when the needed response is to reduce the weight of the snow already there.

A dramatically different approach involves moving into a type of performance mode and trying to crank up the teacher charisma. In this picture, we try to win our students over to our classroom program by increasing the sheer energy in our own teaching. Unfortunately for our students and for all teachers, a major cultural force—cinema—emboldens those who would attempt this route. Think for a minute about the generations of teachers (and, to some degree, students) whose ideas about good classrooms have been formed in part by the film *Dead Poets Society* or other films in that genre. Doubtless, someone as intense or funny or enigmatic as Robin Williams could keep the attention of a group of high-schoolers who might otherwise be distracted. While these students might indeed grasp the importance of seizing the day, whether they would achieve the learning outcomes specified in the curriculum might well remain another matter. This illustrates one approach to overcoming the forces in the classroom: trying to run a classroom where there is never a dull moment (Green Spaces, Chapter 7). I say *trying* because this approach does not even suit the personalities of most teachers, and those of us whom it might suit would likely wear ourselves out after 15 minutes of instruction in that mode. And the curriculum question would remain.

When I use clips from teacher films in my own classes with pre-service teachers, I remind them that the classrooms portrayed in feature films differ markedly from real classrooms, and that *real teachers* and what some call reel teachers might be two different species (Nederhouser, 2000; Reynolds, 2007). Given most reel teachers' lack of training in curriculum, instruction, and assessment, the actors pretending to be teachers might not succeed in actual classrooms at the same rates they do in Hollywood classrooms. Finally, in relation to *Dead Poets Society* in particular, few of us possess either the intensity or the comedy skills Robin Williams possessed. Those disclaimers notwithstanding, the movies still send the message that raw force of personality or a surplus of personal charisma can overcome the natural forces at work in the classroom.

Teacher films illustrate another inadequate response to classroom forces, one unrelated to the comedic chops of a famous funny-man. *Dead Poets Society* and many other teacher films perpetuate the ultimately dangerous image of the teacher as hero (Ayers, 2001). As opposed to most real teachers, who do make sacrifices for their students, cinematic teachers often make extraordinary sacrifices to ensure that no child is left behind. In *The Freedom Writers*, Hilary Swank portrays Erin Gruwell's real-world sacrifices to make certain her students had all they needed (Gruwell & The Freedom Writers, 1999). *Stand and Deliver* brought to the screen the story of Jaime Escalante, the extra-ordinary teacher first introduced by Jay Matthews in his book *Escalante: Best Teacher in America* (1986). I am not the only one to call this hero image dangerous (along with Ayers and many others, such as Dalton, 2004; Farber, Provenzo, & Holm, 1994; Farhi, 1999; Heilman, 1991; Lowe, 2001; Schiff, 2009). This is because this image offers teacher overwork as the solution to teacher overwork. Granted, a late night of work here and there might temporarily transfer some classroom forces to the educational ground. But, if the teacher burns out, overwork will ultimately prove not to have served either the teacher or the students well.

Finally, another common but still inadequate way that teachers might respond to classroom forces is to try to become friends with their students in the hopes that such friendship will cause students to join them on the educational journey. Doubtless, a friendly classroom climate contributes to many students' willingness to work. But *friendship* with students crosses a professional boundary and might backfire.

### Wise and Workable Ways to Transfer Classroom Forces

Implementing the design principles, I describe throughout this book will help teachers to transfer classroom pressures to the ground. Along with a large company of educational researchers, I have concluded that students' own sense of learning power increases when they understand clearly the main point of each segment of their learning (Chapter 3: Strong Centres) and when they can distinguish what belongs and what does not belong in the unit that they are currently studying (Chapter 4: Boundaries). Their self-efficacy increases when they find clear and winsome ways into and out of their topics of study (Chapter 5: Entrances and Exits) and when each topic connects in obvious ways to the rest of their course (Chapter 6: Coherence and Connection). Chapter 7 is especially germane to the question of dealing with classroom forces; we take breaks in life and we need to do the same in school; like us, our students need places to breathe so that they do not feel like they are continuously pushing a freight train. I ground my argument that students need a place of their own (Chapter 8) on the premise that we all need privacy. But the privacy principle connects to the question of forces as well. Some students view their elective assignments, which together become a unique route through the course, less as school-work and more as a kind of retreat. In Chapter 9 (Repetition and Variety), I argue that we need to use repeated structures so students feel safer among familiar assignments, assessments, and routines, and that we vary routines to prevent boredom (theirs and our own). The gist of my argument in Chapter 10 (gradients and scale) is that students' sense of their ability to manage their own learning—that is, their sense of their learning power—increases if we present difficult and massive sections in the right ways. Chapter 11's thesis on piecemeal growth and organic development relates to reducing the pressures felt by teachers inasmuch as our pedagogical burdens become slightly lighter when we are freed from the burden of master-panning for perfection.

Students who find internal motivation for their school-work feel reduced pressure themselves and reduce their teachers' need to push. Teachers have available several means of generating this kind of motivation. First, recognizing students' energy trajectory for the weeks of each unit and working with it simplifies the transfer of forces (Parrish, 2005; 2008; in Chapter 14, I come back to his work). To summarize Parrish's argument, students have more energy for learning some days than others, and we need to take those variations into account when we design and plan units. Most educators know from experience that Parrish is correct in his conclusions about fluctuating student energy. My application here is simple: if we work with rather than against the forces at work in our classrooms, we can reduce the pressures on ourselves and our students. The energy trajectory is likely the closest thing to the arched bridge. Classroom forces are real and substantial, and they naturally need to reach the ground, so teachers need to design structures that simplify and shorten the path for those forces to follow.

We can also transfer forces—reduce pressures—by letting our curriculum and instructional designs show. To brace skyscrapers against wind forces, most architects build thick concrete walls or hide diagonal steel beams in the core of the building, usually around the elevator shafts. Taking cues from the *structural art* philosophy of Fazlur Khan, architect Bruce Graham braced the Sears Tower (called the Willis Tower since 2009) against the legendary Chicago winds by building a frame of nine square tubes, each on caissons reaching down to bedrock and each bolted to its immediate neighbours. The Willis Tower acts as a single edifice. However, structurally, it remains nine distinct towers and, to my point about letting students see the structures of our instructional design, the viewer can easily distinguish each of the nine.

In his design of another Chicago landmark, the John Hancock Center, Graham again rejected the received wisdom of hiding the wind-bracing, this time by putting it on the outer surface of the tower. The Bow, a skyscraper in Calgary, Alberta designed by Foster and Partners (of the UK) and Zeidler (of Calgary), used a similar design (Figure 12.10). One might expect tenants to negotiate lower rent for the inconvenience of large, angled steel beams in their offices in buildings designed like The Bow or Graham's Hancock Center. However, the original landlords of the John Hancock Center found they were able to charge more, arguing that being that close to the building's structure was worth more money.

We can also transfer forces—reduce pressures—by letting the curriculum and instructional structures show. Many teachers show their students the published standards or program of studies as part of their explanation and justification of their instructional plans. Doing so has more than one effect. It does give students

**FIGURE 12.10** Visible, diagonal wind-bracing on The Bow, a skyscraper in Calgary, Alberta

insight into the structure within which their teacher is trying to work in a given year or unit. It also sends the message that teachers see themselves not so much as their students' judge or monitor, but more as their coach and supporter whose job is to help their students produce their best possible work. In doing so, it builds classroom community and encourages both teacher and students to use the pronoun *we*, rather than *you*. In the language of psychologist Carl Rogers, it casts teachers more as *co-learners* with their students (1969), working together to understand what Parker Palmer called *the big subject* (1983, 1998).

Having shown the students the program of studies, curriculum map, or pacing guide, the teacher can increase class ownership of the learning outcomes and reduce pressure by inviting students to contribute their own ideas to the process of unit design. In Chapter 13, I advocate that teachers mess around visually in their design and planning of units, along the lines of my citation from Frank Gehry in Chapter 11. Inviting students into the design process increases their sense of control over their learning (Druin, 2002; Ronteltap, Goodyear, & Bartoluzzi, 2004) and thereby transfers some of the classroom force to the ground. For each upcoming unit throughout the year, some teachers assign a different group of students the task of reviewing the previous year's unit outline a few days in advance of that unit's start date. Their job involves responding to the kinds and weights of assignments, the kinds of instructional activities, and the due dates in relation to other school events. In such cases, not only does the structure show; students are actively invited into the design process. One teacher I know told me she decided to become a teacher the day her teacher assigned her to be part of such a group. An hour of unit design and her interest was hooked.

Some teachers build margin days into every unit. These can function as green spaces (Chapter 7) but the teachers who use them view them more as "Plan B" days. These teachers plan margin days toward the last third of the unit in anticipation of the unanticipated. Unexpected assemblies and fire drills happen. Other disruptions to instruction happen. And students fall behind. By definition, teachers cannot plan for such occurrences, but they can plan days when they can make up for them. Margin days transfer year-scheduling pressure to the ground by helping teachers end teaching units on the days they planned to end them.

Except in the most unusual circumstances, teachers never get away from the reminders of the daily tasks involved in their jobs. But *A Vision with a Task*, a book title from a few decades ago, artfully links those tasks to the idea of vision (Stronks & Blomberg, 1993). The point of the title is that a vision with no identified tasks remains a dream. But a to-do list a mile long with no vision becomes drudgery. While educators have no need to be reminded of the work they must do, they hunger for reminders of the larger vocational picture of which they are a part. In view of that hunger, I recommend that teachers take steps outside their classrooms to develop ways to relieve the direct pressures of classroom life and the larger vocational forces they find themselves facing. First, consider the growing and nearly unanimous bodies of (overlapping) research on the benefits of professional learning communities and collaborative planning (Binkhorst, Handelzalts, Poortman, & van Joolingen, 2015; Gibbons & Brewer, 2005; Huizinga, Handelzalts, Nieveen, & Voogt, 2014; Penuel, Fishman, Yamaguchi, & Gallagher, 2007; Simmie, 2007). Colleagues in a professional learning community walk with teachers through the joys and sorrows of teaching, while helping them design powerful units and improve as professional educators.

For induction teachers (the first five years), mentoring has emerged as perhaps the most important factor in retention. The literature on mentoring and retention is surveyed capably in Hollabaugh's dissertation (2012). Some teachers identify and master a signature method, course or unit with the aim of presenting or blogging about it. Others set a research agenda that leads toward advanced qualifications in a speciality or to another degree. Of direct concern to teachers who find classroom forces daunting, some build systems for every process they know they will need to repeat year to year. Examples include these: term start up, book distribution, attendance, taking in student work, communication with parents, organization of school email. Systems increase efficiency and efficacy and, to my point in this chapter, they transfer loads to the ground.

## Conclusion

The forces that act on contemporary classrooms are as real as the loads on roofs and bridges. For millennia, designers of those structures have worked to find ways to transfer weight to the ground. In the case of bridges and taller buildings, wind adds another design challenge. To meet the challenges facing them, engineers, architects, and designers have produced some unsafe structures and some structures that, to be blunt, are simply ugly. But they have also produced some structures of great beauty, some of them simple in design and some incorporating highly complex engineering and sophisticated materials. Some people consider some of these structures to be works of art in their own right.

Educators can list the forces that act on classrooms in general and they can list the loads that they carry in their particular classrooms. Some of those loads are constant, such as managing the big five (curriculum, instruction, assessment, classroom climate, administration) with a class of 26 students. Some forces hit like a gust of wind on a skyscraper, such as a sudden jump in attendance to 38 students, a head-lice outbreak, or the death of a teacher's family member (all while handling the big five). Teachers need structures to handle the average forces, and they need to know where to find the right supports for the wind gusts.

This chapter began more than a decade ago when I first saw a photograph of Robert Maillart's Salginatobel Bridge (Figure 12.7). The clean, elegant design got me thinking initially about the kinds of forces bridges must handle. Then I thought about the forces that act on classrooms and the structures teachers need to transfer those forces to the ground. I remain convinced that those educators who are willing can learn something valuable from roofs and bridges. In the short term, designing and building the structures I have described will improve student learning. Long-term, designing and building those structures will reward teachers with both vocational satisfaction and improved mental health.

## References

Acland, J. H. (1972). *Medieval structure: The gothic vault.* Toronto: University of Toronto Press.

Ayers, W. (2001). A teacher ain't nothin' but a hero: Teachers and teaching in film. In P. B. Joseph & G. E. Burnaford (Eds.), *Images of schoolteachers in America* (2nd ed.) (pp. 201–209). Mahwah, NJ: Lawrence Erlbaum.

Billington, D. P. (1979). *Robert Maillart's bridges: The art of engineering.* Princeton, NJ: Princeton University Press.

Binkhorst, F., Handelzalts, A., Poortman, C. L., & van Joolingen, W. R. (2015). Understanding teacher design teams: A mixed methods approach to developing a descriptive framework. *Teaching and Teacher Education,* 51, 213–224.

Dalton, M. M. (2004). *The Hollywood curriculum: Teachers in the movies* (2nd ed.). New York: Peter Lang. [Note that chapters 1, 2, 3, 4, 5, 7, 8 are available online through *Education Research Complete.*]

Druin, A. (2002). The role of children in the design of new technology. *Behaviour and Information Technology,* 21(1), 1–25.

Farber, P., Provenzo, E. F., & Holm, G. (Eds.). (1994). *Schooling in the light of popular culture.* Albany, NY: SUNY Press.

Farhi, A. (1999). Hollywood goes to school: Recognizing the superteacher myth in films. *The Clearing House,* 72(3), 157–159.

Fitchen, J. (1981). *The construction of Gothic cathedrals: A study of medieval vault erection.* Chicago, IL: University of Chicago Press.

Gibbons, A. S., & Brewer, A. K. (2005). Elementary principles of design languages and design notation systems for instructional design. In J. M. Spector, C. Ohrazda, A. Van Schaack, & D. Wiley (Eds.), *Innovations to instructional technology: Essays in honor of David Merrill.* Mahwah, NJ: Lawrence Erlbaum Associates.

Gimpel, J. (1993). *The cathedral builders.* London: Pimlico.

Gruwell, E., & The Freedom Writers. (1999). *The freedom writers diary: Stories from the freedom writer teachers and Erin Gruwell.* New York: Broadway books.

Heilman, R. (1991). The great teacher myth. *American Scholar,* 42, 417–423.

Hollabaugh, J. (2012). *Exploring the perceptions and experiences of inductive teachers in secondary education: How do inductive teachers "find their place" in the teaching profession and what motivates them to remain in the field?* (EdD Unpublished doctoral dissertation). Newberg, OR: George Fox University.

Huizinga, T., Handelzalts, A., Nieveen, N., & Voogt, J. M. (2014). Teacher involvement in curriculum design: Need for support to enhance teachers' design expertise. *Journal of Curriculum Studies,* 46(1), 33–57.

Levy, M., & Salvadori, M. (1992). *Why buildings fall down: How structures fail.* New York: Norton.

Lewis, T. (2013). *Divided highways: Building the interstate highways, transforming American life.* Ithaca, NY: Cornell University Press.

Lowe, R. (2001). Teachers as saviors, teachers who care. In P. B. Joseph & G. E. Burnaford (Eds.), *Images of schoolteachers in America* (2nd ed., pp. 211–225). Mahwah, NJ: Lawrence Erlbaum.

Matthews, J. (1986). *Escalante: Best teacher in America.* New York: Holt.

Nederhouser, D. D. (2000). *Reel teachers: A descriptive content analysis of the portrayal of American teachers in popular cinema.* (Doctoral dissertation). Northern Illinois University.

Palmer, P. (1983). *To know as we are known: A spirituality of education.* San Francisco, CA: Harper.

Palmer, P. (1998). *The courage to teach.* San Francisco, CA: Jossey-Bass.

Parrish, P. E. (2005). Embracing the aesthetics of instructional design. *Educational Technology,* 45(2), 16–25.

Parrish, P. E. (2008). Plotting a learning experience. In L. Borruri & T. Stubbs (Eds.), *Handbook of visual languages for instructional design: Theories and practices* (pp. 91–111). Hershey, PA: Information Science Reference.

Penuel, W. R., Fishman, B. J., Yamaguchi, R., & Gallagher, L. P. (2007). What makes professional development effective? Strategies that foster curriculum implementation. *American Educational Research Journal,* 44, 921–958.

Reynolds, P. J. (2007). *The "reel" professoriate: The portrayal of professors in American film, 1930–1950.* Unpublished doctoral dissertation. Bloomington, IN: Indiana University,

Rogers, C. R. (1969). *Freedom to learn.* Columbus, OH: Merrill.

Ronteltap, F., Goodyear, P., & Bartoluzzi, S. (2004). *A pattern language as an instrument in designing for productive learning conversations.* Paper presented at the EdMedia: World Conference on Educational Media and Technology.

Salvadori, M. (1980). *Why buildings stand up: The strength of architecture.* New York: Norton.

**FIGURE 12.11** Santiago Calatrava's Alamillo Bridge in Seville, Spain. His bridges are famous for their lightness and elegant lines

Schiff, P. (2009). Teachers in the movies: Inspirations and care givers. *Kentucky English Bulletin*, 58(2/3), 15–20.

Selye, H. (1956). *The stress of life*. New York: McGraw-Hill.

Selye, H. (1974). *Stress without distress*. Toronto: McClelland and Stewart.

Simmie, G. (2007). Teacher design teams (TDTs): Building capacity for innovation, learning and curriculum implementation in the continuing professional development of in-career teachers. *Irish Educational Studies*, 26(2), 163–176.

Stoddard, W. S. (1966). *Monastery and cathedral in France. Medieval architecture, sculpture, stained glass, manuscripts, the art of the church treasure*. Middletown CT: Wesleyan University Press.

Stronks, G., & Blomberg, D. (Eds.). (1993). *A vision with a task: Christian schooling for responsive discipleship*. Grand Rapids, MI: Baker.

Swift, E. (2012). *The big roads: The untold story of the engineers, visionaries, and trailblazers who created the American superhighways*. New York: Mariner/Houghton Mifflin.

Wilder, T. (2004). *The bridge of San Luis Rey*. New York: HarperCollins.

**FIGURE 13.1** Design elements and age combine in a large, public space to produce privacy and warmth

# 13

# AGILE UNIT DESIGN

In Chapters 3 to 12, I described a pattern language comprising ten principles that, used together, simplify planning and deepen student learning. In this chapter I outline the method for planning a unit that incorporates that pattern language. In order to *get to it*, so to speak, I will begin by listing the steps, and then I will walk through the steps again with brief explanations. Any rationales or discussions of the steps not already stated or implied in Chapters 3 to 12 appear later in this chapter. The steps entailed in this method divide into six sections: Prepare, Catalogue, Plot, Identify, Fill, and Finish.

In several workshops, I have watched in-service and pre-service teachers follow these steps and, in about two hours, design a plan for a unit several weeks long. I use the phrase *agile design* in the chapter title because teachers need quick and flexible ways to design units.

This chapter is packed with instructions and your understanding of it will increase significantly if you actually plan a unit instead of simply reading. Actually, take two hours and plan a unit that you need to teach in the next few months. Plan the unit while working through the chapter, and in two hours or so, you will have a unit design that will simplify your day-today planning. I further recommend that you do this with one or two colleagues.

## Assumptions

Before we get to the steps, let me enumerate here seven assumptions I make in this chapter. First, when I present the design and planning ideas that follow, I have in mind class periods of 40 to 90 minutes. Depending on the grade level, teachers typically break such periods into two or three segments, including time for students to work on their own.

Second, as I have noted repeatedly in this book, designing is only the first part of planning; the steps outlined here have us sketching and messing around the way artists and designers do. I view the day-to-day preparation for teaching as equivalent to building, that is, as distinct from designing and planning. This chapter focuses on design and planning, not on building. Still, as in architecture, the pedagogical building rests on the foundation of design and planning.

Third, for the sake of simplicity, in what follows I assume a unit with four instructional weeks and one extra-long weekend, but the principles apply in any length of unit. Fourth, this four-week unit could be for either a subject-based curriculum or an integrated curriculum. The pattern language works the same way in either setting. Fifth, whether the unit at stake here is integrated or subject-based, as I noted above in my comment on the first assumption, I assume that the teacher in question will provide some time in every class period for students to work. The row of repeated "W"s in the calendar in Figure 13.2 represents students' work time (which, in Chapter 9, I recommended be scheduled at varying times on different days).

Sixth, real-life events happen in teachers' lives during their teaching of any unit, some of those events outside school, some inside. Teachers' family members have medical visits, practices, tournaments. Teachers themselves have meetings, events to attend, shopping, and weekend trips. This design approach to unit planning takes those life realities into account. The bottom row in the calendar in Figures 13.2 and 13.3 reminds teachers to incorporate personal commitments into the unit design.

Finally, what follows relates to planning only one unit. It does not take into account that many elementary teachers teach 7 or 8 subjects per day and that many secondary teachers teach 4 classes. To refer to the sixth assumption and

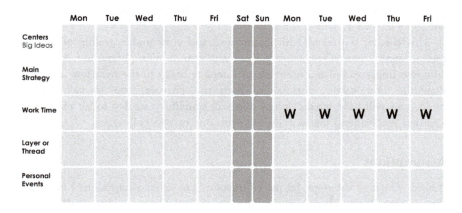

**FIGURE 13.2** A legal sheet, oriented to landscape, showing two weeks of instructional days, with daily work time indicated in the second week

# AGILE UNIT PLANNING STEPS

1. Prepare
   a. Unit design as a collaborative task
   b. Unit design as an aesthetic task
   c. Unit design as a tactile task: Designing on paper, not on screen
   d. The centres
   e. Gathering materials and resources

2. Catalog
   a. Strategies for frequent use
   b. Strategies for infrequent use
   c. Your signature strategies
   d. Textbook's resources
   e. Resources in the teacher guide
   f. Catalogues of strategies
   g. Resources from the internet

3. Plot
   a. Your own commitments
   b. Major dates in other courses
   c. The student engagement curve
   d. The main divisions in the unit
   e. The centres
   f. The unit's main entrance and exit
   g. Internal entrances and exits
   h. The most difficult elements

4. Identify
   a. Through-lines
   b. Adjustments from the last time you taught the unit
   c. Green spaces
   d. Threads and layers
   e. Major assessment points
   f. Minor assessment points
   g. Public and private places

5. Fill
   a. Repeating specific teaching-learning strategies
   b. Using a variety of teaching-learning strategies
   c. Varying the use of class time
   d. Clarifying the boundaries

6. Finish
   a. Transfer the contents to a computer

revert to internet slang momentarily, teaching IRL (*in real life*) implies that other teaching responsibilities and plans will impinge on the unit one is designing for a given period of time. Plotting one's real-life schedule onto a working calendar is an important part of the second stage of this process; big days in other courses and classes are clearly part of planning IRL as well. For example, anyone scheduled to start a new unit on the 10th of the month knows that students will not get next-day service on major assignments they are scheduled to submit on the 9th of that month; I assume here that on the evening of the 9th the teacher is engaged in unit design and planning.

In the section that follows, I offer more detailed explanations of the above steps, referring briefly to the concepts presented in Chapters 3 to 12. At the end of this chapter, I offer two lengthier discussions of matters included in this list. The first of those relates to what Patrick Parrish (2008) has called the student engagement curve (Step 3c here). The second connects to my argument that unit design differs from unit planning and must precede it (Steps 1b and 1c here).

## 1. Prepare

**Summary:** This stage includes two moments or movements: understanding the design task and gathering resources and materials.

a.  Unit design as a collaborative task
    Recent research shows that teachers plan better units when they plan with one or more grade-level or subject-area colleagues (Voogt, Pieters, & Handelzalts, 2016). Consider this seriously.
b.  Unit design as an aesthetic task
    Contemporary educators have become so accustomed to starting planning with the big idea (to use the language of McTighe and Wiggins) that many of us experience a kind of visceral resistance to approaching it any other way. Here, I ask you to approach designing and planning this one unit in an aesthetic frame. Let us treat the design of this unit as a design task, not strictly a cognitive task.
c.  Unit design as a tactile task: Designing on paper, not on screen
    Those among us who are not professional graphic designers—which I assume includes almost all educators—will design more effectively on paper than we will on software. For this design task, I recommend two legal sheets, taped end to end, so that you can see the whole four weeks of the unit at once. If you wish, print two copies of a simple table (as in Figure 13.2) in your word processor. This process is done on paper, but some steps require you to keep a computer handy.
d.  The centres
    What are the main divisions of the unit? How are the weeks of the unit divided up? These divisions can reflect the big ideas and learning outcomes

but do not do so necessarily. At this point, use a pencil to indicate the main time and topic divisions within the unit. We will return to this matter in the Plotting stage of the process (steps 3d and 3e).

e.  Gathering materials and resources
    Instructional materials come from many sources, a few of which I list here.

- Load any templates or materials your jurisdiction provides.
- Scour the internet for 15 minutes, looking for other teachers' related lessons or even whole units. Copy links to the sites into an open file in your word processor. At the time of writing, the string "California lesson plans water cycle science" yielded nearly 12,000,000 records and "Ontario lesson plans Canadian geography grade 5" yielded 3,000,000. From the results, flag at least one lesson for each of the major sections in your unit. This will save you significant time in the short term. You can adapt and customize this material organically year by year and make it more your own with time (as discussed in Chapter 11). Year by year, teachers drop or adapt their borrowed materials, but induction teachers especially must give themselves some breathing space when building their classroom programs.
- If there is a textbook, have it handy, even if you know it well. Examine the textbook to see how it has organized the material. If you wish to revise your list of big ideas, do so now, recognizing that the text is merely one resource, not the law. Also recognize that younger students might assume that the textbook's organization of material has a kind of quasi-legal status.
- Skim or scour the textbook for more instructional ideas. For example, some teachers address their students' reading skills by having them read a page or two in their textbooks and, for each of the paragraphs on those pages, identify what question each paragraph answers. Teachers have come up with thousands of similar strategies; we just need to find out about them.
- Have the teacher resource guide for the textbook handy. This suggestion re-appears in Step 2e below.
- Download or open The Ontario Curriculum Unit Planner: Teaching Learning Companion. This is an encyclopedia of teaching-learning strategies of the sort many ambitious teachers want to assemble; they realize they don't need to once they see this resource. https://faculty.nipissingu.ca/darleneb/Relevant_links_docs/telrsta2002.pdf

## 2. Catalog

**Summary**: Every teacher has a repertoire of strategies. In this step, you remind yourself of that repertoire and identify places to expand it.

a.  Strategies for frequent use
    On small sticky notes, identify four or five major teaching-learning strategies (methods) that you know how to use well and can use at least three to four times during this unit (Repetition and Variety, Chapter 9). These frequent-use strategies should include relatively brief and brisk activities that you can intersperse between more major activities. Examples might include such popular approaches as these: jigsaw (also known as home groups/expert groups), think–pair–share, three-column SOS (summary–opinion–support) sheets, three-column PMI (plus–minus–interesting) sheets, and reading circles. Write each of these on separate sticky notes and indicate for each whether you consider it a low-, mid-, or high-engagement strategy, writing the names of the highest-energy strategies on brightly-coloured sticky notes. We rank these for engagement levels because on days when student energy is lower, we need more engaging strategies. Note that not all phases of a given strategy have the same energy level. For example, jigsaw can be quite high-energy while students prepare their material but rather low-energy and even boring when they deliver their material (as children with no teacher-training tell each other what they know by using direct instruction).

b.  Strategies for infrequent use
    On sticky notes, identify four or five more strategies (methods) that you know how to use well but will use only once or twice during this unit. This category includes activities that take more preparation. For example, student presentations require two or more periods of preparation beforehand, plus the class periods during which students present. In view of those time requirements, you would likely never use presentations more than once in a unit. Rank these strategies for energy levels. As you identify these strategies, note again which of them usually result in the highest levels of student engagement.

c.  Your signature strategies
    Identify the most powerful strategies that you will use no more than once each and will use only on the key dates in this unit. As you did in Step 2a, write these on bright sticky notes.

d.  Scouring the textbook
    Even if you are familiar with the textbook, look at it again for instructional ideas. Identify on sticky notes major topics on which it provides information, questions, activities, assessments, and any other food for thought related to each of the major sections of the unit you distinguished in Step 1d. Many textbooks are custom-published to suit precisely the learning outcomes or program of studies of a specific jurisdiction. During the writing and production phases of such publications, publishers are in constant conversation with the respective department of education and likely employ teachers from that jurisdiction to work with them on an editorial team. Due to all the careful work that has been put into them, textbooks can serve as essential resources for teachers and their students.

e. Checking the teacher resource guide
Most publishers publish a teacher resource guide to accompany the textbook. What instructional ideas does it offer that you have not used before? Write these on sticky notes. If you have not been in the habit of purchasing these resource guides, now is the time to start.

f. Catalogues of strategies
Using the table of contents of the *Ontario Curriculum Planner* or your preferred encyclopedia of strategies, identify 1 or 2 new teaching-learning strategies you will pilot in this unit. Because new strategies take more time to organize than familiar ones, plan on one or two hours extra of preparation for the single class session in which you pilot a new-to-you strategy.

g. Raiding the internet
In the preparation stage (1e, second bullet), I suggested raiding the internet for materials. As you do, keep your eyes open for teaching strategies, too.

## 3. Plot

**Summary**: This stage involves plotting on your paper calendar your personal time commitments, major events in other courses, the overall schedule of this unit, the students' predicted energy trajectory for the weeks during which the unit runs, and landmarks within the unit.

a. Your own commitments
Mark on the calendar (as in Figure 13.3) any weeknight commitments you already have scheduled that will affect how much time you can work on the Monday through Thursday nights during this unit. Except in cases where the cat in the hat shows up to help, most educators do not accomplish any school work on a weeknight when they also have a concert or evening

| | Mon | Tue | Wed | Thu | Fri | Sat | Sun | Mon | Tue | Wed | Thu | Fri |
|---|---|---|---|---|---|---|---|---|---|---|---|---|
| **Centers** Big Ideas | | | | | | | | | | | | |
| **Main Strategy** | | | | | | | | | | | | |
| **Work Time** | | | | | | | | W | W | W | W | W |
| **Layer or Thread** | | | | | | | | | | | | |
| **Personal Events** | | Parent Interviews | Parent Interviews | | | | | | | Concert | | |

**FIGURE 13.3** Two of the four weeks of the unit, with personal commitments and major events in other courses plotted on the bottom row

meeting. Next, mark weekends on the calendar where your personal commitments will prevent your working for most or all of the weekend.

b.  Major dates in other courses

Mark on the calendar any evenings before major dates in other courses. For example, planning and designing a unit that begins on the 16th in another course (the major date) implies that the evening of the 15th is available only for that design and planning, not for anything in this course. Similarly, taking in major student assignments in another course usually implies an evening of grading. On the calendar, mark the dates when such work is coming in. Do not schedule to take work in that you cannot grade; students get anxious over the delay, and their asking when they will get it back makes most teachers feel guilty and frustrated.

c.  The student engagement curve

Using a coloured marker or pencil, indicate what you expect will be the student engagement curve over the weeks during which the unit runs. This draws from the work of Patrick Parrish (2008), who has also produced worthwhile work on other questions of instructional design (2005, 2009). Veteran teachers know that learning-energy drops on Fridays and does not fully recover on Mondays. On long weekends, it drops for two days before and takes two days to recover. Also, student absences increase on both sides of long weekends, forcing teachers to find creative ways to continue instruction with those in attendance while not making them feel punished for being there. Figure 13.4 illustrates a typical energy curve. A longer discussion of the engagement curve appears toward the end of this chapter.

d.  The main divisions in the unit

Step 1d focused on the centres, big ideas, and main divisions of the unit. By default, educators often schedule these intra-unit divisions with only the jurisdiction's standards, pacing guide, or program of studies in view. If the curriculum specifies four major sections for the unit, then we usually divide the time available (roughly) by four. Of course, responsible educators recognize the quasi-legal nature of the curriculum in place. This approach makes complete sense. But a borderland—a field for give and take—exists

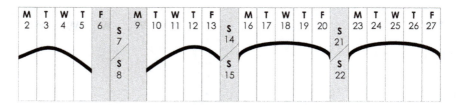

**FIGURE 13.4** The student engagement curve for four weeks, during which there is a four-day weekend

between the standards and the student engagement curve. Start new things on days when student engagement runs higher. End things at times that fit the natural rhythms of students' lives. Employ higher-voltage strategies when you expect student energy to be lower.

e.   The centres

Identify a strong centre within each of the main time divisions of the unit (Chapter 3). These centres may be major concepts, major bits of instruction, or major assessments, field trips, simulations, or culminating activities—that is, any higher-energy activities. Students know that such activities are the hinge around which the unit swings; they are the centres of the design. These centres warrant your most engaging strategies.

f.   The unit's main entrance and exit

The unit should start with the kind of high-impact activity that generates learning energy (Chapter 5, and here, Figure 13.5). If the unit starts on a day when student energy will be low, then the teacher needs to bring extra energy by means of one of the high-voltage activities listed on a bright sticky note from steps 2a, 2b, or 2c.

Recall from Chapter 5 the teacher who started her France unit with the trip to Paris in a wide-bodied jet. The clear entrance activity (such as a new unit outline) lets students know they have moved to a new section of the course. The grand, engaging, wonder-inducing invitation (such as an imaginary flight to Paris) might lead the students to wonder if this will be the most amazing unit they have ever done in their lives.

In one workshop, some teachers suggested starting the unit on the water cycle with a trip to the river. Yes, on day one! The skeptical teacher wants to ask, "But what about scaffolding their learning to get maximum value from that trip?" The inquiring teacher responds, "But why not start inquiry by inquiring?" For my money, a trip to the river sounds more interesting than "Turn to page 168 in your text and do questions 1–5." The last day of the unit should be equally notable and memorable, a real exit from the unit. Inevitably, some units will end with a unit test, but we should move away from that as a default setting.

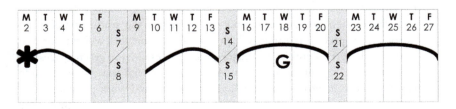

**FIGURE 13.5** An asterisk on the first Monday indicates a grand entrance to the unit. The teacher's design includes a planned green space on the Wednesday of the third week of the unit

g.   Internal entrances and exits
Each sub-section of the unit should start with higher energy (Chapter 5) and should not end with a whimper. As was true of the main entrance, if a sub-section starts on a day when student energy is typically low, the teacher will need to compensate.

h.   The most difficult elements
Note on the calendar which are the most difficult lessons conceptually and which are the most massive sections of the unit. Plan to introduce those parts in stages and to hide some of the mass. Set back the most difficult elements (Chapter 10). Design the unit so the instruction on these areas lands on those calendar days that you predict students will come with more learning energy. Typically, students require scaffolding for such sections, and you should indicate on the calendar how many days you expect to direct to these more difficult segments of the unit.

## 4. Identify

**Summary:** The next steps continue the plotting process begun in the above section.

a.   Through-lines
Identify the through-lines. I explained this term in the discussion of coherence and connection in Chapter 6. Even a unit of four weeks needs to be tied together, especially when the specified learning outcomes, while conceptually connected, may seem to students to be spread all over the map.

b.   Adjustments from the last time you taught the unit
What changes do you need to incorporate that you noticed the last time you taught this unit? Great courses are built with the help of several cohorts of students (Chapter 11, Master Plans and Organic Development). If you have not been in the habit of making written or digital notes to yourself along the lines of "Change this next time," then start making those notes now.

c.   Green spaces
Because four weeks or more can be a long push for you and your students (especially when no long weekends occur during the unit), identify one major green space in the unit (Chapter 7). For a unit that will run for five weeks or longer, identify two major green spaces. Major green spaces are at least one class period long, sometimes two. Green spaces can include video, resource centre/library time, games, guests, and work periods. In the skeleton unit represented in Figure 13.5, a long weekend offers both teacher and students a green space after just four days of instruction. The letter "G" in the middle or end of week three represents a green space declared by the teacher in light of design principles.

Identify several minor green spaces and space them out between the major green spaces. These can include work time every day and shorter bits of video or music incorporated into instruction. Depending on their content, some threads and layers (Chapter 6) can play important instructional roles and simultaneously function as green spaces.

If in step 2a you identified some relatively brief or brisk activities to intersperse between more massive parts, these could serve as green spaces as well (Chapter 10: Gradients, Harmony, and Levels of Scale; Chapter 9: Repetition and Variety).

d.  Threads and layers

Layers are those activities that repeat daily or almost daily. They can be distinct for 5–10 minutes per class or embedded in other instruction. Threads happen every two to three days and take less time than layers (Chapter 6: Coherence and Connections; Chapter 9: Repetition and Variety). You cannot do it all, so identify just one thread or layer that you will build into each instructional day during this unit. Read and talk with your colleagues about how to vary the contents within that thread or layer.

As I noted in Chapter 6, threads and layers can include literacy, numeracy, current events, the plants and animals in the room that need care, exploring multiple intelligences, music, local geography, art, tech skills, video clips, meta-cognition, weather, learning styles, physical activity, social skills, social intelligence, and many more matters worthy of classroom time. For many teachers, work time every day is the one non-negotiable layer; students and their teachers both need it.

e.  Major and minor assessment points

Identify two or three minor assessment points and one or two major assessment points and mark them on the calendar. Recall why the phrase *formative assessment* became popular: major assessments should not always happen on the last day of the unit or on the last day of each sub-section of the unit.

f.  Public and private

Identify components of the unit—especially in assessment—where students will be able to choose what work they complete to create a private space and still meet the unit's learning outcomes (Chapter 8: Private). Identify what instruction and assessment the class will experience in common (Chapter 8: Public). Some of the common experiences should be uncommon; identify some common experiences what will be special and celebratory.

## 5. Fill

**Summary:** With the standards or program of studies and your resources/strategies inventory in front of you, identify the activities for the other instructional days.

a.  Repeat specific teaching-learning strategies
    Used at the right frequency, familiar learning strategies provide students with a measure of security (Chapter 9: Repetition and Variety). Identify on which days you will employ the strategies with which your students are most familiar.

b.  Varied teaching-learning strategies
    Ensure that you vary your use of teaching-learning strategies (Chapter 9). Strategies such as think-pair-share become popular because students respond well to them, but we must not use them every day. Remember your own repertoire, and remember to keep your own brain alive by creating one new lesson or implementing one new strategy every year in every unit (Chapter 9).

c.  Vary the use of class time
    Variety applies to the segmenting of class time as well. Work time should be moved from the start, to the end, to the middle of the period. You could even have it both at the start and the end, to signal to students that you are not stuck. Vary the length of class segments. The truth of the engagement curve idea is that every day cannot be spectacular. In music, *allegro* and *adagio* work in combination. Students need a parallel experience in class; they need both intensity and quiet.

d.  Clarify the boundaries
    Make clear not only the entrances and exits, but also the boundaries (Chapter 4) so that students know what belongs and what does not belong in the unit. The simplest boundary markers are printed unit outlines. A posted schedule that shows all instruction and student work leading to a culminating activity also works.

## 6. Finish

**Summary:** We transfer the results of our manual, tactile, paper-based designing and planning onto a computer.

a.  The large sheet of paper provides a literal overview of the unit. Transferring the contents of the messy design sheet into a computer file requires shifting from visual and aesthetic modes of thought back to the usual ways teachers think: about preparation for instruction, about epistemology and the structures of disciplinary knowledge, about psychology and learning theory, and about adaptations and accommodations for exceptional students. Transfer the results of your design process to your computer, taking joy in the new discoveries you made about pedagogical territory with which you may have been quite familiar.

## Closing Discussions

### *The Student Engagement Curve*

Earlier in the chapter, I credited Patrick Parrish (2008) for having identified and explained the engagement curve (Figure 13.4). In my view, Parrish has identified the simple reality that educators and students have more energy for the work of teaching and learning some days than others, and that teachers should design and plan instruction accordingly.

A couple examples illustrate how I have adapted Parrish's idea and incorporated it into unit design. Either voluntarily or involuntarily, a teacher frequently ends up with a week-night commitment that starts just after dinner and runs until near bed-time. A mid-week play or concert, parent interviews, and board meetings are all examples of these commitments. This kind of evening activity affects the next day's instruction in at least two ways, both of which are obvious but also easy for idealists to forget. First, there is less time or none at all for either grading or planning the next day's work when one is otherwise occupied in the evening. And second, as important or enjoyable as such an evening might be, one likely goes to work somewhat tired the next day, which is an example of lower teacher energy that is rather easy to predict. Weekend travel for the teacher produces the same result the following Monday.

Students' energy for learning is influenced by some of the same factors and in the same ways. They may well arrive in our classes excited about what they have been learning in the last few days or by what we have lined up for them today. The cliché example of course is the 7-year old studying dinosaurs. But our students also give their attention and energy to their music, their sports, their drama events, their love lives, their hobbies, their service trips, their jobs, their clubs and voluntary involvements, and, of course, their family commitments, some of them involving travel and some of them involving rough home and neighbourhood lives. And, like us, on the days just before a long weekend our students are not at their most focused for academic work.

There is little wisdom in viewing students' activities outside school as a distraction or a negative; these are just part of life. Likewise, school is just one part of an educator's life, not all of it, and this reality ought to push educators to design instruction in view of the real rhythms of their own lives and the lives of their students.

Chapter 10's discussion of organic and piecemeal development implies a caveat for any educator plotting an engagement curve: our plans and predictions will not be perfect. We cannot know exactly how much learning energy our students will bring to class each day for the next four to six weeks. For that matter, we cannot even predict our own energy. I recommend the excellent book *The Energy to Teach* by Donald Graves (2001), but predictability remains outside his reach as well. Energy in a single room is significantly influenced by the classroom teacher, but world and local events also affect energy levels, as do wins and losses in sports, the lives and health of individual students' family members, and even announcements from the school office.

Finally, every class has a certain ethos, what the educational databases call classroom *climate*. Teachers are the biggest influence on the classroom ethos and, with their students (but largely under their own direction) they build one kind of ethos or another every school year from the first day of school onward. That ethos can be characterized by more or less curiosity, more or less noise, more or less learning from mistakes, more or less reading, more or less respect, more or less anxiety, more or less anticipation, more or less inquiry, and so on, depending mostly on the cues teachers give and how skilled they are at responding in a thousand moments so that a positive climate is built. My point here is that in an ongoing way throughout the school year, a classroom ethos has more or less energy; the engagement curve is not a function only of the day of the week or the proximity of a long weekend.

## Unit Design or Unit Planning?

These two points appeared as steps in the preparation stage in the list at the start of the chapter: *Unit design as an aesthetic task* (Step 1b) and *Unit design as a tactile task to be done on paper, not on screen* (Step 1c). I include these claims and provide the discussion below because, as I argued in Chapter 1, the default approach to planning for most educators is to frame planning either in our knowledge of our students (both as cohorts and as individuals) or in our knowledge of the curriculum and the learning outcomes our jurisdiction has specified. Some decades ago, this debate became known as *the logical vs. the psychological*. Some joke about it with the false binary *I teach subjects vs. I teach students*. The language may change from one decade to the next and one staff room to the next, but the contours of the argument remain roughly the same. To my point, neither view expressed in this false binary encourages educators to start planning instruction by thinking first about designing instruction.

In our own time, educators have become so accustomed to starting planning with *the big idea* (to refer again to the language of McTighe and Wiggins, 2005, 2013) that many educators experience a kind of visceral resistance to approaching it any other way. In their defense, starting with the word *design* instead of with the word *planning* is, for many, like speaking a foreign language. Earlier in the chapter, I gave only a few lines each to the two statements related to design as an aesthetic task and a tactile task. I offer here a quick tour of the ideas about the aesthetic and tactile features of design on offer from a sampling of artists, designers, and architects.

Three themes or arguments appear in the discussion of design as a process best done on paper: speed, simplicity, and the generation of new ideas. The first theme, more of a cluster of ideas, relates to the speed of designing on paper.

Paper allows the designer to make on-the-spot changes. Rough sketches allow the designer higher initial production speeds compared to the time most people need to produce similar drawings on a computer (Kivett, 1998). The authors of one study on software design (unironically) list among the "affordances of paper" that paper allows the software designer to see "information at a glance" (Sellen & Harper, 1997, pp. 1, 8).

The second argument, which is related to speed, is the simplicity of using paper compared to using software. Teachers need to focus on the design and planning, not on how software works. In Hokanson's words, planning with simpler media such as paper is superior because simpler media "impose less of their own structure on the interchange and allow a freer form of idea development" (2008, p. 86).

The third and more fundamental theme that runs through this discussion is that designing on paper actually generates new insights. I will call this the *epistemological argument* for using paper, that one can understand the project or problem only by engaging in design. One finds this idea throughout the design literature, that messing around on paper and sketching not only *help* one to represent what one already understands but they also bring about new understanding. In fact, sketching is indispensable to thinking in design

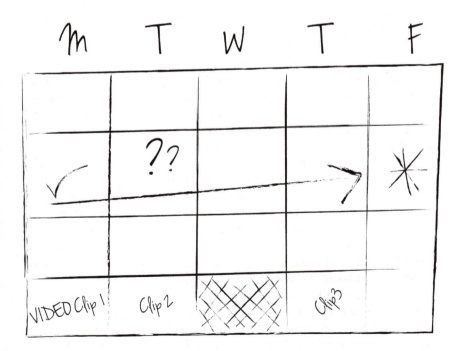

**FIGURE 13.6** Unit design begins with messy exploration

fields. In Goldschmidt's words, "the designer does not represent images held in the mind . . . but creates visual displays which help induce images of the entity that is being designed" (1991, p. 123). Goldschmidt, in fact, uses a concept that educators may want to consider, that as one attempts to sketch or design a unit, the difficulties in creating that sketch provide a kind of *backtalk* to the designer. Interpreting and responding to this backtalk leads to improvements in the design and to deeper understanding of the ideas one is attempting to develop in the sketch (Goldschmidt, 2003).

Goldschmidt is not alone in holding this view about how designers use backtalk. In a 1996 interview, Donald Schön, whose name most readers of this book will recognize because of his concept of reflective practice, discussed how designers' sensitivity to backtalk or even a kind of conversation with backtalk can lead to unexpected discoveries (Schön & Bennett, 1996). According to Schön, the designer's response to the difficulties encountered in design generates design surprises. This idea is consistent with how he describes reflective practice. Others echo this view. Koper, for example, writes that "educational design needs to be seen as a process in which a designer makes a number of more or less tentative design commitments, reflecting on the emerging design/artefact and retracting, weakening or strengthening commitments from time to time" (Koper, 2005, p. 7). Note that in Koper's hands, design is iterative; we play and we mess around. One writer has called that freedom to play one of "the virtue[s] of paper" (Hokanson, 2008). With many others, he argues that drawing itself facilitates and sharpens thought. Fraser and Henmi use language quite similar to Hokanson's and Schön's; for them, "drawings eliminate and reduce in order to clarify and increase understanding" (Fraser & Henmi, 2008, p. 161). A few pages later, they claim that "Drawings stir new conceptions through their marks on papers, ideas that exist because of and through the material presence of the drawing act. In this sense, they're both representations and origins, that which comes to be represented through other means" (p. 164).

This chapter is not the right venue to review this conversation exhaustively. However, I do recommend the works of several others among its participants, all of whom have argued one way or another that making and thinking—that is, designing and planning—have become separated and must be relinked, and that we must figure out our plans as we design (McAndrew, Goodyear, & Dalziel, 2006; McKim, 1980; Schwartz, 2016). Those interested in reading further along this line should see Fraser and Henmi's book, as well as Pallasmaa's *The Thinking Hand* (2009). Although he focuses on craft more than on design, Matthew Crawford's best-selling *Shop Class as Soul Craft* (Crawford, 2009) serves as a very readable argument in this same genre. Interestingly, when it appeared in Britain, its American title was changed to *The Case for Working with Your Hands*.

What are we to make of this idea, especially those of us who are more inclined to get to planning right away, instead of designing first? In my workshops,

## VISUAL PLANNING

Planning visually works because it allows us to pick an area of study and create an engaging task that will enrich student understanding. Throughout my teaching experiences, I have realized that one area of study connects to many other areas of study. Therefore, when planning visually for a specific unit, it is easy to think of engaging tasks that will hook students into the learning process and develop their intrinsic motivation to learn. I believe that this planning process helps educators develop relevant, relatable, realistic and authentic tasks that promote problem solving and critical thinking in the classroom. It also puts engagement at the front of each area of study planned. This, in turn, helps facilitate inquiry-based learning and allows for student voice and choice.

K. MacIsaac

I have watched both pre-service and in-service teachers make discoveries because they showed sensitivity to backtalk. I have heard a teacher blurt out, "This won't work there, because of what we're doing the next day!" Granted, such discoveries could be made while planning on-screen, in a word-processor file. But when working on paper and designing—when focusing on design—instead of simply planning, one becomes more sensitive to the backtalk, which enables one to make discoveries and understand new ideas.

One pre-service teacher who participated with me in several workshops described how using these principles to design first—and then plan—made sense to her (please see the "Visual Learning" box above). She had already become proficient in lesson-planning through the course work and practicum placements entailed in an excellent education program. But designing first transformed how she understood and approached planning.

Educators need to take this conversation seriously. We should design on paper not so we can see what we already think, but so we can think new things. Unless we are also professional designers who use computers all the time for design tasks, our best designs will likely come to us when we mess around on paper. Yes, we must think about the program of studies, the standards, and the learning outcomes. But let us start by messing around. Design is an iterative process. Great designs often start on the backs of envelopes, at least according to legend. In both mythology and real life, many steps and many people intervene between the envelope and the finished product. We need to awaken the visual, not because we do not believe there are psychological and epistemological aspects to planning, but because playing around visually will reveal to us new ideas and will contribute to improvements in what our students finally study.

## Conclusion

A common complaint of K-12 teachers is that the daily demands of teaching practice prevent their engaging with educational theory. Teachers know they need to undergird their work with ideas, and they also know that ideas that never get put to use are, in a sense, useless. Throughout this volume, I have tried to show how the principles of design theory land on the ground and how they actually advance and simplify the day-to-day work of teachers. More than any other, this chapter has focused on how to build an actual unit in light of the ten principles I developed in Chapters 3 to 12.

Teachers always tweak and adapt the resources they find, and I know that the ideas in this chapter will be expressed and realized in forms I cannot imagine. I welcome the prospect of creative teachers adding to the steps I have outlined here (and subtracting from them) to simplify and streamline their classroom work further, and to bring new levels of agility to their planning. I do not view this chapter as the last word on the process of designing units. But neither is it the first word. In honesty, the first words on unit design came from the hundreds of architects and designers who worked long before any of us began teaching.

## References

Crawford, M. B. (2009). *Shop class as soulcraft: An inquiry in the value of work.* New York: Penguin.

Fraser, I., & Henmi, R. (2008). *Envisioning architecture: An analysis of drawing.* New York: Wiley.

Goldschmidt, G. (1991). The dialectics of sketching. *Creativity Research Journal*, 4(2), 123–143.

Goldschmidt, G. (2003). The backtalk of self-generated sketches. *Design Issues*, 19(1), 72–88.

Graves, D. (2001). *The energy to teach.* Portsmouth, NH: Heinemann.

Hokanson, B. (2008). The virtue of paper: Drawing as a means to innovation in instructional design. In L. Botturi & T. Stubbs (Eds.), *Handbook of visual languages for instructional design: Theories and practices* (pp. 76–89). Hershey, PA: Information Science Reference.

Kivett, H. A. (1998). Free-hand sketching: A lost art? *Journal of professional issues in engineering education and practice*, 124(3), 60–64.

Koper, R. (2005). An introduction to learning design. In R. Koper & C. Tattersall (Eds.), *Learning design: A handbook on modelling and delivering networked education and training* (pp. 3–19). New York: Springer.

McAndrew, P., Goodyear, P., & Dalziel, J. (2006). Patterns, designs and activities: Unifying descriptions of learning structures. *International Journal of Learning Technology*, 2(2–3), 216–242.

McKim, R. H. (1980). *Experiences in visual thinking.* Boston, MA: PWS Engineering.

McTighe, J., & Wiggins, G. (2005). *Understanding by design* (2nd ed.). Alexandria, VA: Association for Supervision and Curriculum Development.

McTighe, J., & Wiggins, G. (2013). *Essential questions: Opening doors to student understanding.* Alexandria, VA: ACSD.

Pallasmaa, J. (2009). *The thinking hand: Existential and embodied wisdom in architecture.* Chichester, UK: Wiley.

Parrish, P. E. (2005). Embracing the aesthetics of instructional design. *Educational Technology,* 45(2), 16–25.

Parrish, P. E. (2008). Plotting a learning experience. In L. Borruri & T. Stubbs (Eds.), *Handbook of visual languages for instructional design: Theories and practices* (pp. 91–111). Hershey, PA: Information Science Reference.

Parrish, P. E. (2009). Aesthetic principles for instructional design. *Educational Technology Research and Development,* 57(4), 511–528.

Schön, D., & Bennett, J. (1996). Reflective conversation with materials In T. Winograd (Ed.), *Bringing design to software* (pp. 171–184). New York: Addison Wesley.

Schwartz, C. (2016). Critical making: Exploring the use of making as a generative tool. *Journal of Curriculum & Pedagogy,* 13(3), 227–248.

Sellen, A., & Harper, R. (1997). *Paper as an analytical resource for the design of new technologies.* Paper presented at the CHI '97: Human Factors in Computing Systems conference, Atlanta, GA.

Voogt, J. M., Pieters, J. M., & Handelzalts, A. (2016). Teacher collaboration in curriculum design teams: Effects, mechanisms, and conditions. *Educational Research and Evaluation,* 22(3–4), 121–140.

**FIGURE 14.1** Groin vault shows the patina of long use. Its arches offer users an enclosed space

# 14
# CONCLUSION

In the foregoing, I have offered a justification for approaching unit planning through a design frame. I have listed ten principles which, taken together, comprise a language. Any of the component parts of this language will simplify planning and enhance student learning. Used together, they have a multiplier effect on both planning and learning. In Chapter 13, I outlined the steps involved in planning a unit according to these principles. In this last chapter I offer a brief argument for the scalability of these principles, a short annotated reading list, and a brief conclusion.

## Scalability

If the design principles reviewed in Chapters 3 to 12 apply to the design of units, they should also apply to the design of individual lessons. That is, they should scale downwards without difficulty. They should also be scalable upwards, to courses and to a whole curriculum. I have focused throughout this book on designing the unit, theme, or topic, but will turn here to the smaller element, the class, and to the two larger entities, the course and the curriculum.

### The Class

Many teacher-training programs require their pre-service teachers to use a lesson-planning template. To their credit, most of these templates require the teacher to begin by identifying the desired learning outcomes for the lesson— the big idea or big question—before identifying the activities the lesson will involve. In the early chapters of this book, I expressed satisfaction that educators have moved toward an approach to planning that starts with the learning outcomes, then identifies the assessments, and then plans the instruction. However, I also noted that my satisfaction remains incomplete; I flagged a concern in those early chapters that the backwards-by-design approach will not necessarily produce unit designs that fit teachers' and students' actual lives or that fit with the rest of the course of which they are part. In short, I faulted conventional planning approaches, including backwards-by-design, for jumping straight into planning without designing first.

Ignoring design may harm lesson-planning as well. We need a lesson-planning model that takes variations in student learning energy—even during a class as short as 40 minutes—into account. As there is an energy trajectory or learning curve over a week, over a unit, and over a year, there is also one during a single period. If we plan a lesson as if that lesson were our students' only activity in a given day, our lesson-planning templates might work perfectly. But these planning templates tend to be decontextualized, and we need to remember that the particular class that we're planning is situated in a point in the day, after some other activities or after a break, and before some other activities or before a break. These immediate contextual factors affect the success of our lesson-planning. The pattern language I have offered in this book applies to lesson-planning (and I invite my readers to lead the way on articulating the specifics of those applications).

## *The Course and Curriculum*

The principles I have offered in Chapters 3 to 12 also scale upward to whole courses and to whole curricula. Because this is not a volume on course and curriculum design, I will treat this as briefly as I did day-to-day planning in the two paragraphs above. Asking "What is the big idea" or "What is the centre?" is a bigger necessity at the course and curriculum level than at the day-to-day level. Bad planning or haphazard instruction that wastes our own time and that of our students for one period or one day is bad enough. But a wasted course or a curriculum with no apparent point is a travesty. So, to recall Chapter 3, we should identify the respective centres of our courses. I suggested there that we might take up the pedagogical and linguistic challenge of summarizing our course in as few words as possible. Reducing a course in that way helps us remember why we and our students do our work

Connecting to the idea of centres, I argued in Chapter 4 that units need boundaries because students need to know what belongs and what does not belong. So do we. Boundaries help focus attention on the centre. We and our students need to know what belongs in the course, so I argue that the principle of clear boundaries applies to courses as well. In curriculum-planning committees and in academic advising, we also need to know the boundaries of the curriculum. Welding programs in technical schools have the singular goal of producing a graduate who can weld and, one assumes, with that goal always in view, they

**FIGURE 14.2** The Novel Hart stationery design illustrates scalability. Themes run throughout, from the smallest pieces to the largest

protect their curriculum ruthlessly. They may be a model for all of us who serve at some point on a curriculum committee. I argued earlier in the book that entrances function as the corollary to boundaries. This is true of courses and curricula as well. If we are going to establish course and curriculum boundaries, then we need to make clear to students the locations of the ways in and out. Students need to know when and where they start, and how and where they can finish.

Chapters 7 and 8, on green spaces and the private/public continuum, connect to courses more obviously than they do to whole curricula. I argued in Chapter 7 that teachers and students need spaces in which to step back and breathe. In Chapter 8, I asked that we create private places for students by allowing them to fashion work of their own. These principles apply to courses. In Chapter 8, I also noted that courses tend to default toward common or *public* modes of instruction and learning but that we may not recognize the opportunities there to design celebration into our plans. This argument also applies to whole curricula. Programs should have times of public celebration. The Mount Royal University program in which I teach, for example, has a major science fair in the third year and a major capstone exposition and reception in the fourth year. Students look forward to and back on these events. The capstone fair draws co-operating teachers, recruiters from school districts, parents, and many others from other departments in the university. Doubtless, some come simply for the food and drink, but most come to celebrate our students' success. Curriculum committees should design such events into their multi-year plans, whether those be events like those I just mentioned, research conferences, public speech or spelling evenings, or any of a dozen other possibilities.

The canonical design principles I mentioned in Chapters 6, 10 and 11 all scale up to the course and the curriculum. A course needs variety and repetition, as does a curriculum. Courses and curricula both need to be designed and built in ways that recognize the need for gradients and human scale. I argued in Chapter 11 that great units rarely result from master planning. Rather, we design, plan, and then teach what we planned, and then we repair and revise in light of how our students responded to what we brought. Like graphic design, unit design is iterative; we come back and back and back. Courses work the same way. Some veteran teachers complain when they hear curriculum revision mentioned; after all, they were probably part of the last curriculum revision. A bit like the junior-high student who, when confronted with yet another unit on democracy, complains, "We already did this," a seasoned educator may fail to recognize that there are good reasons to examine the curriculum again, even though the last revision may have been only a few years ago. Curricula may be a form of master-planning, but they improve through organic growth as educators and students use and inhabit them year after year.

Finally, I argued in Chapter 12 that we should design our units using smart, simple structures. The same holds for courses and curricula. This connects to my argument in Chapter 3 that we should identify the centre so that we and our students can focus our work. Light, simple structures should undergird our courses and whole curricula.

As I closed my brief discussion of how these principles scale downward to the individual class, I invited my readers to take up the challenge of articulating exactly how that might work. I repeat the challenge here with reference to whole courses and to curriculum revision. These have not been my focus in this book but if these principles are in fact worth following and can bring real improvement to unit design and planning, then others (in addition to me) should take up the challenge of seeing how they apply on the larger scale. I mentioned the attempt by Robert Yinger to implement a pattern language in the design of teacher-training curriculum in the 1980s (1989). The time has come to attempt this again.

## The Unit

For nearly a century and a half, the unit has had a central function in the thinking of K–12 educators. But it has not caught on to the same degree in higher education. Professors are not the primary intended audience for this book, but I will note here that the concept of the unit could revolutionize instruction in higher education. K–12 teachers know how unit-planning works. Designed as I have described them here, they work better. The unit would help students in higher education for the simple reason that it breaks their semester's work into parts, some of which can fit the natural divisions of the semester (long weekends and reading breaks). The corollary is that the professor's planning is broken into the same parts; in units there are starts and stops to topics. I will not argue this further here but will again offer the challenge—this time to higher educators—to try this approach to course design.

## Conclusion

As long ago as 1897, in *The Decoration of Houses*, Edith Wharton lamented that the decoration of houses had been disconnected from their design; decorators and architects had gone their separate ways. She argued that anyone decorating a house had to work in harmony with the structure of the house, not simply adding elements for their own sake, which, by virtue of their disconnection from the structure, would thereby appear superficial. In her view, decoration had to follow the fundamental lines of the room. She even went so far as to argue that if the design were good, then the materials used in decoration would not be as important. Teachers know that the materials used (the parts of the curriculum) are important, so I am prevented from accepting her whole argument here. But I do want to go this far: if the design is good, and if we have made clear to our students the purpose of what they are learning, then the day-to-day activities will fit into a whole and our students will be more motivated to learn and more capable of learning. Our designing and their feeling like powerful learners ultimately connect. We must design before we plan and build. And we must make good designs. Our students deserve no less.

## References

Wharton, E. (1897). *The decoration of houses*. New York: Norton.
Yinger, R. J. (1989). *A pattern language for teaching (a planning/working document for the School of Education)*. Cincinnati, OH: University of Cincinnati.

**FIGURE 14.3** An inviting space built on many of the design principles described in Chapters 3 to 12

# AUTHOR BIOGRAPHY

Ken Badley
Education Department
Mount Royal University
Calgary, Alberta
kbadley1@gmail.com

**Dr. Ken Badley** teaches educational foundations at Mount Royal University in Calgary, Alberta and serves as Professor by Special Appointment at Tyndale University in Toronto, Ontario. Immediately prior to teaching at Mount Royal University, he taught in the doctoral program in education at George Fox University in Newberg, Oregon from 2007 to 2016. Before teaching at George Fox, Dr. Badley taught from 1975 to 2007 in three Canadian provinces at the secondary, undergraduate and graduate levels. His current research interests include how teachers gain, maintain, lose, and share classroom authority, and the intersections in classroom instruction between Csikszentmihalyi's concept of *flow* and van Manen's concept of *tact*. He has been involved in textbook projects for several Canadian provinces and has worked extensively with teachers in Kenya.

# INDEX

CPSIA information can be obtained
at www.ICGtesting.com
Printed in the USA
LVHW011326250821
696067LV00016B/2086